on

Greenhill
Books

Cracking the Luftwaffe Codes

Cracking the Luftwaffe Codes

The Secrets of Bletchley Park

Gwen Watkins

Foreword by Asa Briggs

Greenhill Books, London
MBI Publishing, St Paul

Greenhill
Books

Cracking the Luftwaffe Codes
The Secrets of Bletchley Park

First published in 2006 by Greenhill Books/Lionel Leventhal Ltd,
Park House, 1 Russell Gardens, London NW11 9NN
and
MBI Publishing Co., Galtier Plaza, Suite 200, 380 Jackson Street,
St Paul, MN 55101-3885, USA

British Library Cataloguing-in Publication Data

Watkins, Gwen
Cracking the Luftwaffe codes : the secrets of Bletchley Park
1.Watkins, Gwen
2.Great Britain. Government Communications Headquarters – History
3.World War, 1939–1945 – Great Britain – Cryptography
4.World War, 1939–1945 – Electronic intelligence – Great Britain
5.Bletchley Park (Milton Keynes, England) – History
I.Title
940.5'48641'092

ISBN-13 978-1-85367-687-1
ISBN-10 1-85367-687-X

Library of Congress Cataloging-in-Publication Data available

For more information on our books, please visit www.greenhillbooks.com,
email sales@greenhillbooks.com, or telephone us within the UK on 020 8458 6314.
You can also write to us at the above London address.

Edited and typeset by Wordsense Ltd, Edinburgh
Printed and bound in Great Britain by Creative Print and Design (Wales), Ebbw Vale

For David Wendt

Without whose generous help and prodigious memory this book could never have been written

Dear David,

In those far-off days when we were both young and both at Bletchley Park, you seemed to me to have one fault: you were absurdly modest. You never seemed to realise that other people could not have done the things that you did, nor have made the discoveries that you made. And now, in your eighties, you still have that fault.

When the Defence Signals Directorate (DSD) awarded you the Australia Day Medallion for your 'numerous "firsts" in a very difficult area', your 'rare ability to assimilate and correlate minor pieces of information', the 'originality and accuracy' of your research, which 'contributed significantly to DSD's high standing in the SIGINT community', you said that the medallion might have gone to a chauffeur or cleaner – it just happened to have come round to you.

But your employers knew better. When you retired, they said that during your twenty-two years in the DSD you had acquired the reputation, not only in your own organisation but also in many others, of being an expert in your own field and for being responsible for many significant achievements in that field. It was the same at Bletchley, wasn't it? You did extraordinary things, and always thought that anyone else might have done them.

So, do you believe now that you were brilliant, and that no one else could have done what you did?

No, of course you don't.

GMW

Contents

Illustrations

Foreword

by Asa Briggs

EVERYONE WHO WORKED at BP (Bletchley Park) during the Second World War – and our numbers are diminishing – had her or his secrets, and everyone by oath was bound to keep them. For reasons that she explains, Gwen Watkins in her fascinating memoir now feels that she can tell some of the secrets of a unique establishment that during the war scarcely dared to speak its name. In the absence of written archives, memoirs are of crucial importance, and time is running out.

At BP I was in a different section from Gwen's, but I met her there and knew well the man whom she married, the poet Vernon Watkins. Through my own experience I can confirm that the details which she sets out in her clear and highly readable account of her own experience at BP are authentic. I greatly admire her skill in putting everything together.

At the time both of us were very young – Gwen describes herself as 'young and silly' – and both of us reacted sharply against the pretensions of 'authority'. These were never entirely missing in BP, but there was a strong sense of common participation. Once inside BP you came to feel, as she comments, that it was a 'social place'. Even before its secrets began to be told I had come to the conclusion that it needed a good social history.

To me BP, after Cambridge, was an education in itself, both in working and in living. Gwen and I were carrying out different tasks. In military uniform I was a cryptographer working in Hut Six on the Enigma cipher, a member of 'the Watch'. 'Intelligence' was separate from cryptography, although I was a member of the Intelligence Corps and that gave me cover when I was outside. As a WAAF (Women's Auxiliary Air Force), Gwen was employed in breaking what we called 'low-grade' Luftwaffe codes. I was unusual in knowing more than most in BP about what other people were doing. I had friends in many sections, including people who were working on more difficult ciphers than Enigma.

I knew at the time how essential to the effective work of BP – and to the winning of the war – was the work of WAAFs, WRNS (Women's Royal Naval Service) and the ATS (Auxiliary Territorial Service). I had never seen so many women in my life! Even then, though muzzled, I dreamed of writing a history of BP, more than a social history, just as Gwen dreamed of writing a novel. Vernon actually wrote poems, and there were lots of future publishers around. Both my history and Gwen's novel would have dealt with the relationships (a crucial word at BP) between men and women. Both would have focused also on the relationships between the younger and the older members of the BP community. The older were not very old, but they seemed old to us. Indeed, this was my first sense of 'a generation gap'. Because BP was a 'sociable place', formal and informal relationships mattered. If I were writing my history or my autobiography I would concentrate on them more than on functional charts of responsibilities.

Gwen's account speaks for itself, but for me she makes three main points about BP which are not often made. First, the experiences of the people working there are only part of their lifetime experiences: there was a before and after. This comes out vividly in what is said in her book about David Wendt and, indeed, about GCHQ (Government Communications Headquarters). Second, people's experiences at BP encompassed their life outside BP as well as inside it. Their billets, which varied widely in the facilities and amenities that they offered, were as much the scene of their lives as the architecturally interesting offices in which they worked, and a pub, like the Duncombe Arms at Great Brickhill, lingers as much in the mind as the refectory in BP itself. The Bletchley cinema too played a big part in all our lives. Third, the American presence at BP, late in manifesting itself, affected everyone who worked there. I was on the Watch in Hut Six when Bill Bundy and his colleagues arrived. Previously I had met Telford Taylor, a soldier who made his mark as an historian. I had met very few Americans before 1942, and it was by spending a lot of time at their headquarters that I first learned of tomato juice, American bacon, American coffee and, not least for me, American universities. I kept in touch with Bundy and some of his colleagues after the war. New relationships had begun, and they subsequently unfolded. One of my closest American friends, Frank Stanton, married a girl who worked near to him at Bletchley. Their family in sociological terms was a by-product of BP. Frank was a pop song writer, who had taken a degree in English at Yale, and through him I came to learn about Broadway and Nashville, Tennessee.

It did not much matter what subjects one had studied before going to BP. People who had read English could be just as good cryptographers as people who had read mathematics. In my own part of Hut Six – the Machine Room, which was separated from the Watch – we had to know about all the properties of the Enigma machine. Alan Turing was on the edge of my world. I made my own way to BP by a circuitous route, with the mathematics Fellow of Sidney Sussex College, Cambridge, Gordon Welchman, watching me on the way. He appears frequently in Gwen's account, and he wrote a book about BP, *The Hut Six Story*, which got him into trouble. He was a critic of authority.

Far from getting into trouble with *Cracking the Luftwaffe Codes: The Secrets of Bletchley Park*, Gwen Watkins will pass into general history, and not just the history of cryptography and of Intelligence. I am proud to have been asked to write this foreword to her book. I am grateful to her for writing it.

Introduction

WHEN WE CODE-BREAKERS left Bletchley Park on or before VE Day (8 May 1945), we found on our Certificate of Discharge a warning. This is what it said:

You are hereby reminded that the unauthorised communication by you to another person at any time of any information you may have acquired whilst in His Majesty's Service which might be useful to an enemy in war renders you liable to prosecution under the Official Secrets Act.

We younger ones looked at this with awe and respect. It seemed to set the seal of secrecy on our work at the Park. It really did not occur to us that these certificates were printed by the million, and that every Service man and woman had an identical one. In any case, we needed no reminder that we must never speak of the work we had done at the Park. We had been too deeply indoctrinated for that; so for years it has been habitual to us not to reveal anything about the time we had spent there. We had learned how to fend off questions from family and friends by saying when asked what we did, 'Oh, routine paper-work, you know', or we relied on the fact that most people would rather talk about themselves than about anything else on earth. In spite of the huge posters everywhere saying 'Careless Talk Costs Lives', a great many people, human nature being what it is, did chatter rather carelessly; but we never did. There were probably some strains in this; but silence soon became a habit, and, like other habits, it was difficult to break.

It had never occurred to us, either, that this silence could ever be broken. We had made friends at Bletchley, often for life, and many of us had married a colleague. Naturally after the war we often talked about our friends there and off-duty incidents, but never, as far as I know, did any of us mention the work we had done, even to our partners. It was as though it had never existed. By far the greater number of BP workers had never heard of the Enigma codes or their secret product Ultra, which, historians say, did so much to shorten the war. Then in 1974 F. W. Winterbotham's book *The Ultra Secret* revealed that GCCS (Government Code and Cipher School) had succeeded in breaking the Germans' most secret ciphers, which they had thought impregnable. This threw us into complete confusion. Had the ban on speaking out been lifted? Was our total silence no longer necessary? There was certainly no public announcement, although in January 1978 the Foreign

Secretary stated that people who had given 'undertakings of reticence' about 'Enigma/Ultra' were released from them to a limited extent. Most of us knew nothing of this announcement, and certainly had no private communication from our former masters; so we still kept silent. Some, especially the older ones, maintained that the oath taken by the signing of the Official Secrets Act was for life, and could never be broken. And many of them did keep silent, till death and after.

Then, in 1982, followed *The Hut Six Story* by Gordon Welchman, one of the chief code-breakers of the Enigma codes. This revealed a great deal about Enigma. It was reasonable to assume that he had been given permission to make these revelations, and so he had, but in a very British way. The government had certainly cleared him, but GCHQ had not. A close colleague has stated his opinion that Welchman was 'ridiculously persecuted on security grounds for revealing, some forty years after the event, how the job of breaking the Enigma had been done.' I do not myself think that this was the reason, or at least the sole reason, why he was 'persecuted'. At any rate, it was of no use locking the stable door now that the horses were out and galloping away.

Books on Bletchley Park and its work were then published, notably *Codebreakers: The Inside Story of Bletchley Park*, and the book of the Darlow Smithson TV programme *Station X* in 1998. In hardly any of these books was it suggested that anything of importance went on except the breaking of Enigma codes. But if that were so, what were all the thousands of us, the great majority, doing for the years that we worked eight-hour shifts with one day's leave a week, for a derisory sum, if what we had done was of no value, not worth recording?

For the four-hour television programme I was interviewed and filmed for several hours, and doubtless others were filmed as extensively; but none of us except those who had worked on Enigma appeared for more than a few seconds. In the book of the film, the section on which I worked, German Air Section, does not even appear in the index. There is a short article in *Codebreakers*, which suggests that most of the interception and decoding of German Air traffic took place at Cheadle, with minimal input from BP, and that it was in any case valueless. If this were true, then we should have been wasting our time; but I am sure that it is not true. The writer was either poorly informed or mistaken. We few survivors were indignant. 'Somebody should write a book,' we grumbled.

But the TV programme had been useful in one way. My old friend and colleague David Wendt saw it in Australia some months afterwards, and wrote to me, for the first time since the sixties. I still felt something of the awe we young girls had felt before his brilliant intellect. I felt it again when we talked about the war, and it appeared that no detail of our work had disappeared from that phenomenal memory. Not only did he remind me of many things I had forgotten, but he told me about things I had, in my more limited sphere, never known. I was tremendously excited, and urged him to begin immediately on the definitive book about German Air Section; but he had other plans to occupy his eighth decade. He calmly told me it was up to me to write the book, and generously gave me full permission to use any or all of the information he had given me. A short time after receiving his letter, I read Robert Harris's novel *Enigma*, about Bletchley Park, and this really did galvanise me into beginning my own book. I could not bear that readers should think BP was anything like that. Where were the glorious eccentrics, the brilliant wits, the men and women of outstanding intellect, even genius, who had helped to save Britain and, some critics say, to shorten the war by two years?

Of course we humbler code-breakers did not know until many years afterwards how outstanding some of our colleagues were, nor how they had toiled to break the Enigma codes. You might see a scruffy figure, tearing at the skin round his nails, shuffling rather like a crab into the Newmanry. But even if someone who had read mathematics at Cambridge had told you in an awed tone that he was Alan Turing, you would have been no wiser.

After his death a cousin of his asked me if he had really been as eccentric as his biography recounted. I was able to reassure her that he was not much stranger than many of his colleagues ('mad people on all sides', as an army private, Charles Cunningham, said on his first day); and that chaining your mug to the radiator, which seemed specially to distress her, was not really so eccentric. If you had a china mug and it was 'borrowed', you could replace it only by an enamel one, which made tea taste horrid. And cycling to work in your gas mask, if you had hay fever, was a good idea. She seemed relieved, and thanked me very much, assuming that if I had worked at

BP I must have known her cousin. But this was like asking an acquaintance who lived in New York if he knew your cousin in Hoboken. However, everyone did know Hugh Alexander, the British chess champion, since he would give exhibitions in the mansion of playing twenty or thirty simultaneous games; but of the hundreds who watched him perhaps a dozen would know what his work was.

We in the German Air Section did know one or two of the 'pundits': Enid (later Dame) Welsford of the flashing eyes and the fierce temper – if you lit the touchpaper, it was wiser to retire immediately; and dear Josh Cooper, head of the Air Section, whom we were accustomed to see roaming the corridors like a huge grizzly bear, although much more genial. He had a habit, while thinking (and when was he not?) of stroking his left shoulder behind his back with his right hand, into which, through long practice, he had managed to twine the fingers of his left hand. Vernon Watkins, our own German Air poet, once mischievously asked him the time when he was thus entangled, and after an heroic struggle Josh said apologetically, 'Sorry, I'm afraid you'll have to ask someone else.'

But these were the people who were doing so much for the success of the war effort. Perhaps I haven't succeeded in showing how extraordinary those Bletchley years really were. Who could? Regrettably, we had no Boswell there. Every day one learned something new; every day one's perception of life expanded. Well might Josh Cooper say that a year at BP was equivalent to a university degree; but no college that I have ever known could supply such an education. To quote our poet, it was 'a situation, an era and an excitement which cannot be repeated'.

If you visit Bletchley Park today, you will be given a small map showing where everything happened: B Block where Italian air and naval codes were broken; C Block with its huge card index; H Block which contained Lorenz and Colossus – all the huts and blocks appear on this map, with their appropriate work listed alongside. But instead of F Block there appears simply a hollow rectangle described as 'Site of F Block'. It is the only block to have been completely demolished. Its history, its memories and its very self have been demolished too, apparently. Perhaps David Wendt and I are the only people who remember this building when it was alive with the good, the clever, the brilliant and the fascinating who wrestled with the Luftwaffe's own special codes.

When, fifty or more years afterwards, the Trust that now runs Bletchley Park took it over, very likely there was nothing at all left to show that the German Air Section had ever existed. If that is so, this book may add something to the forgotten history of the place without which, so historians say, the progress of the war might have been so different.

Acknowledgements

I AM MORE INDEBTED than I can say, or than anyone would believe, to David Wendt, for his generous and unstinting help and instantaneous replies to my desperate cries for assistance – all this from the other side of the world; and to my son Gareth Watkins, who brought my old-fashioned language up to date, made suggestions for improvements of which 99 per cent were used, and prepared the final disk for the publishers.

Thanks to Michael Leventhal of Greenhill Books for his support and his friendly advice when the book was still in embryo; and to David Watkins (no relation, or there would have been more recriminations than there actually were when, three weeks before Christmas, he sent me a vast packet of corrections, emendations and suggestions to be incorporated into the book. They were all necessary). And, finally, heartfelt thanks to the anonymous Greenhill reader who must have toiled for months to make sure that every tiny historical detail was correct. My deep gratitude to all who helped me so much.

Cracking the Luftwaffe Codes

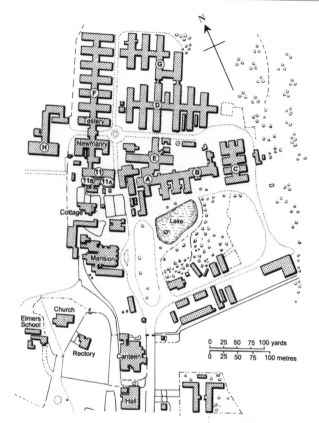

Bletchley Park, 1939–1945

Blocks

A Naval intelligence
B Japanese naval codes; German/Italian Army and Air low-grade codes
C Contained the Hollerith punchcard sorter for the Central Index
D At beginning of 1943, Hut Six moved here. It also contained Q Watch and translators from the Z Watch German naval section, who processed information for the Admiralty

E Main teleprinter room
F (from north): Japanese Army and Air (two spurs); MI6; SALU (a top-secret air-codes consultancy); German Air (two spurs); the Testery; (over the bridge) the Newmanry
G Traffic analysis and deception operations
H The Newmanry moved here in early 1944; Lorenz lived here, as did eventually ten Colossi

Huts 11, 11a and 11b were all devoted to bombes

Chapter 1

In the Beginning

MY FATHER ENLISTED in the Royal Army Medical Corps (RAMC) in 1915, when he was just eighteen. He must have seen appalling sights during the First World War, and have handled men who were suffering terribly, but he never once spoke about his war – to his family at least. I have watched television programmes of veterans from both wars, and they too break down almost at once, and can rarely tell of their experiences. My father possessed a beautiful silver medal given him by the Belgian government for an '*acte de courage et de dévouement*', together with an immense framed testimonial lavishly illustrated with further acts of courage, such as ladies in transparent nightgowns being rescued from burning houses, children being saved from various predicaments, a baby being held out to a mother who was fainting, having obviously thought it dead, and other interesting scenes. This, though an object of inexhaustible fascination to me in my childhood, was never associated in my mind with any part of my father's life.

He remained silent about his war all his life, but his younger brothers said that it had changed him for ever.

I was born four years after his demobilisation in 1919, and I grew up never once reading or hearing about the horrors of war. For me and my contemporaries, war was a subject of romance. We read Ernest Raymond, whose *Tell England* – a bestseller – was about three young lieutenants who went through Gallipoli and France with only the most glamorous of wounds, and who died with noble sentiments on their lips. To John Buchan war was a glorious game; to Ian Hay it meant scenes of muscular laughing Highlanders sitting in the trenches in sunshine, competing on who could kill most 'cooties' from their shirts. J. M. Barrie wrote wistful plays about young soldiers (always officers) waiting 'beyond the veil' for their loved comrades to join them.

We were brought up on the poetry of Rupert Brooke and his fellow poets, who regarded war as a wonderful opportunity to escape from the dullness of ordinary life; but our school anthologies contained no poems by Wilfred Owen or Siegfried Sassoon, who showed war in all its wasteful horror.

We had never seen anything like C. S. Lewis's description of his experiences in the First World War, near Arras. 'Through the winter, weariness and water were our chief enemies. I have gone to sleep marching and woken again and found myself marching still. One walked in the trenches in thigh gumboots with water above the knee; one remembers the icy stream welling up inside the boot when you punctured it on concealed barbed wire . . . The war – the frights, the cold, the smell of

HE (high explosive), the horribly smashed men still moving like half-crushed beetles, the sitting or standing corpses, the landscape of sheer earth without a blade of grass, the boots worn day and night till they seemed to grow to your feet . . .' No, we read nothing like that.

My friends who volunteered immediately for the Second World War, desperate that if they waited they would not get into Air Crew, had, I know, no vision of themselves trapped in a blazing plane, intolerably mangled or burned. We had not even any idea that war could involve ordinary clerical work, cleaning, boredom – war meant to us drama and romance, and we could not wait to take part.

So, resisting all efforts by my teachers and parents to persuade me to stay on at school and go to university, I applied on my seventeenth birthday to join the WAAF and was put on Deferred Service. This meant that you had to go home and wait until one day, without any warning, you were told to report to some distant point. I thought I would earn some money while waiting, and became a temporary clerical officer in the Aliens Department of the Home Office, which had evacuated itself at the beginning of the war to a rather plush hotel on the West Cliff at Bournemouth. This was full of young people like myself waiting to be called up, who had replaced the civil servants of military age who had volunteered or been called up. The elderly higher clerical officers who remained were aghast at the irruption into their hitherto cloistered corridors of this crowd of young people who thought nothing of laughing and talking during working hours, or of rushing down to the basement supposedly in search of a file, but really to gossip and giggle with their friends. Our elders were like flustered mother ducks trying to round up their ducklings. But we had all been well brought up and well educated, and we did do our work; only we did it much faster than it had been done in former leisured days. After working for Higher Certificate exams, the Home Office was a doddle.

My job, which was interesting, was concerned with the 'aliens', most of whom had lived and worked peacefully in Britain for thirty or forty years, and had been suddenly interned on the Isle of Man under the infamous Regulation 18B. There were with them a number of refugees from the growing oppression of the Nazis. These, though most of them were completely innocent, might have been spies sent over by the Germans, and had therefore to be investigated. All the internees were frantic to get back to their businesses and their families, and the volume of correspondence we had to deal with was very large indeed. My job was to open the letters, translate them if necessary, summarise and docket them and hand them on to my boss for evaluation and decision. We did not always see eye to eye.

I remember one day we had an anguished letter from a young Austrian who had escaped, penniless and without luggage, from a place whose name was not at that time as familiar as it was to become after the war – Dachau. It was not then a concentration camp, merely a labour camp where fit men could serve out their prison sentences working for the Third Reich – without pay, of course, and on a nearly starvation

diet, with very brutal guards. According to this correspond-
ent, many men died under this cruel regime, and he would
perhaps have suffered the same fate had he not decided to
get away. He had with great difficulty, and undergoing many
hardships, managed to arrive in England to serve in the war
against the Nazis, only to find himself interned as soon as he
reported himself to the authorities. My boss did not believe his
story, on the reasonable grounds that the Germans, who like
us needed all the manpower they could get, were not going to
treat their workforce so stupidly as to waste it. I pointed out
that that was exactly the argument used by slave owners to de-
fend their workforce, and that Charles Dickens had rubbished
that argument by pointing out that, in all the advertisements
for missing slaves, the description of the runaways showed
that almost all had undergone brutal treatment and suffered
horrific injuries. My boss was a senior civil servant, and not at
all used to opposition from his inferiors; but, staring grimly at
me, he did reread the letter, and reluctantly put aside his big
'R' stamp (for rejection). I pleaded that the young man at least
merited some kind of investigation; and, while meeting my
former boss much later, I heard that the Austrian was serving
in the Pioneer Corps.

But, strangely, a much sterner view was taken of a letter
from a rather whiny young Italian complaining of horseplay
in his hut. He had apparently had his penis painted blue
while deeply asleep one night. My boss immediately scrawled
a docket demanding that the camp commandant at once in-
vestigate this behaviour. He was astounded to see me giggling,

and it turned out that a large part of his indignation was due to the fact that a young lady should be forced to read such disgusting language. There is no doubt that the Civil Service had become somewhat hidebound; and no doubt either that I should never have made a civil servant.

I was called up in 1942, and was sent with another fifty girls to RAF (Royal Air Force) Innsworth, a few miles out of Gloucester. Here we spent three days being kitted out, being taught the rudiments of marching, listening to lectures and learning how to identify an officer, and how and when to salute (never unless both of you are wearing a cap, since you are not saluting a person but the king's commission, represented by the cap badge. Watch out for films about the war, and see how often this mistake is made). As we were all lined up in front of a WAAF officer to give her details of our civilian life, I had the exquisite pleasure of hearing a pleasant girl in front of me, on being asked what her job had been, say 'I was a tart' and seeing the officer's dropped jaw and staring eyes. The girl responded helpfully, 'I don't work from the streets – I have my own flat. And I'm quite high class; I only go with officers.' I never saw that girl again, but if she remained in the Service I should think she would have managed to carry on her former trade very successfully.

On the third day we had to sit Trade Tests. I had always been very good at exams and found them easy, but to my horror I discovered that I could hardly do any of these. I couldn't do mathematical progressions once they got into the twenties; I couldn't fit upside-down shapes into a dodecahedron;

I couldn't see from diagrams how to change fuses or fit fan belts. The only thing I could do was write a short essay on why I wanted to join the WAAF.

The next day the whole intake was sent for six weeks' initial training to Morecambe. Oh, heavenly Morecambe, with not a single tourist desecrating that marvellous bay! I still feel a great nostalgia when I think of it. We were billeted in houses where formerly bathing costumes had hung on the balcony railings and sand shoes dried on the window sills, and we were fitter than we had ever been, exercising all day in the sunshine and healthy sea air. We were trained in drill by a guardsman, and soon recognised the fascination of moving in synchronised figures, like a *corps de ballet*. Where at first we had stumbled and limped on route marches of one mile, by the end of the six weeks we were marching gaily for ten miles, singing all the way.

A group of old men used to follow the various squads about, for the pleasure of seeing nubile young girls doing PT in blouses and shorts. When I was teasing one of these once, he told me that they had little interest in girls, but were waiting to see the Germans invade across the flat Morecambe sands. 'Because then they'll get a surprise, won't they, when they start to sink in the quicksands? And we'll watch 'em go down, and when we sees only their helmets, we'll laugh till we bust!'

On the last day we had a glorious passing-out parade, after which we assembled to hear which trade we were to follow and to which station we were to be posted. I was in deep gloom, because those Trade Tests must have been assessed, and I was afraid I would be put in the lowest (and worst paid) group, the aircrafthands, who did all the menial jobs no one else wanted to do; so I was mightily relieved to hear that I was to be a clerk/general duties, in grade four. Even a clerk could have fun, if you were posted to an interesting station, a fighter or bomber command, or radar, or a balloon site. But oh, what horror, what disappointment! I was posted back to dull old Innsworth, to work in the RAF Records Office!

I was not to know then that this posting would subsequently lead on to another, which I would not have missed for worlds.

Chapter 2
Setting the Record Straight

GLOUCESTER WAS A CHARMING small city in those days, with very little traffic in its old streets, and Beatrix-Potter-like timbered shops all round the Close. Doubtless they were as much infested with mice as the original Tailor's, and they certainly smelled of damp and poverty, but they sold second-hand books and trumpery antiques, and were fascinating to poke through. The city's one defect was that, since it lay in a deep bowl or saucer, surrounded by its lovely hills – Robinswood, Birdlip and Coney – it rested also in a bath of what we should now call smog, because in those days coal was used for every purpose (cooking, heating and industry) except in full summer. A local lady explained its effect to me in this way, 'You see, m'dear,' [all friends, enemies and strangers were 'm'dear'] '. . . you see, we takes in the mist when we'm born, and it don't leave us till our last breath; and so we'm not bright. We'm good-hearted, but we'm not bright.' They were good-hearted, kind, generous and helpful, but they were undoubtedly slow of comprehension; and these were the only people that RAF Records was able to employ as part-time clerks. Many of them had left school at fourteen and worked on farms or as house-wives, and were not really fitted to do clerical work. They were darlings, and would bring home-made cakes in to share with the small number of WAAFs who worked alongside them, and they loved to chat, and they worked quite slowly, finding the filing and sorting rather difficult.

The result was that, although the system of record keeping was simple and in theory should have worked perfectly, its simplicity demanded one essential – that the filing should be kept up to date; and it never was. Most of the ladies had homes and children to go to, and could only work part time, and al-though the small band of WAAFs worked until six o'clock six days a week, we never had enough time. The consequence was that the record cards were always in a muddle.

It should have been as clear as day. In our room we dealt only with airmen below the rank of warrant officer. All offic-ers' records were dealt with in a sacred room never entered by ordinary WAAFs, and aircrew too were dealt with separately (presumably since the huge number of deaths and horrific in-juries were not to be known by the rank and file). So in our room every RAF station had its record cards in a large metal box, called a bin. Each clerk sat at a table with her bin before her, or sometimes the bins of two small stations. Each bin had a number of tall stiff cardboard dividers, filed alphabetically by trade: armourer, baker, cook, dog handler and so on. Each record card had the surname and Christian name of the bearer in capital letters on the left-hand side and his or her trade in capital letters on the right-hand side.

Every morning an 'update' from your particular station was put on your table. It listed every change that had taken place in the personnel of that station: who had been sent to hospital or on a course; who had taken Trade Tests to upgrade his qualifications; who had changed trade; who had been promoted; who had been put on a serious charge. Thus it contributed to all the minutiae necessary for an airman or airwoman's record while in the Air Force. If a person were dismissed or left, you extracted his card from your bin and took it to an LACW (Leading Aircraftwoman) who sat at a table in front of the room. You also took his card out if he had been posted to another station, and the LACW would take it to his new station. She would also bring to your table the cards of any personnel who had been posted to your unit, and you would file them under their trade. So, basically, all you had to do was to enter the details on the update on each record card named in it. Simple. If you knew the name, the trade and the station, you should theoretically be able in a few moments to put your hand on any card needed.

Theoretically. The trouble was partly that the ladies worked part time and would depart in a hurry, often leaving the day's update uncompleted. Then when they came in the next day, they would try to finish the previous day's update, while often having to leave the current day's update unentered, so that they got further and further behind. Then they often forgot to file by trade, and would slip a card in alphabetically somewhere by surname, or if an airman's name were Cook or Baker he might be filed under those trades. So the bins were not up to date, and the cry would frequently go up 'I can't find this card!' You were supposed to cross off the names on the update as you entered the details, and then hand it in to the LACW. (I had thought she looked rather glum when I first saw her; and now I knew why. She was supposed to be the troubleshooter for the room, but there was too much trouble there for any one girl.) The updates had more and more un-entered names on them, because the card could not be found. The WAAFs worked pretty well, and when the ladies were not there we would go round their bins trying to fill in their incomplete updates; but the confusion filtered down to every bin. It was clear that something must be done.

I had found out that you could get promoted by taking tests. They were, unlike the daunting Trade Tests, only applicable to your own trade, and were the sort that I could, as a French friend of mine used to say, do with both hands tied behind my head. So I rapidly became a corporal. Now I had some real authority – not much, but some.

I found the officer nominally in charge of our room, whom we hardly ever saw, because he was in charge of more rooms than he could manage, and told him we needed to reorganise the bins. He told me that on no account must there be any disorder in the bins, as it was vitally important that we should at any moment be able to find any card at all. I took this as a kind of silent permission, and asked him to request from every station the list which it must have of its own personnel, and left before he could raise any objection. In a few days we had our lists, and we could then begin on our reorganisation. The first thing to do was to go round to every bin with its list, and take out every card that should not be there. We put all these cards into a huge bin on the front table. Our little band of WAAFs worked like the devil, coming in after the evening meal, and some even came in for part of their day off. Nobody can have any idea of how many RAF stations there were in Britain in wartime. (We did not, thank Heaven, deal with stations abroad.) In the mornings the ladies cast envious eyes on the huge bin, being convinced that their missing cards were in there, which they undoubtedly were; but they were sternly forbidden to meddle.

At last we began to make progress, and had actually begun to file in their proper bins the formerly misfiled cards, when one Saturday an immensely senior RAF officer came round the various rooms allegedly on a visit of inspection, but really, I think, to fill in a dull weekend. He was of course escorted by our officer and a deferential WAAF officer. He strolled round our tables, and then caught sight of the big bin, still half full, on the front table. He asked what was its function, and looked inquiringly at our officer, who naturally had no idea, and looked inquiringly at me. I said meekly that there were some cards which had accidentally been misfiled, and that we were in the process of filing them correctly. This brought on a very strong reproof to our officer, that it was essential every card should always be in its correct place, otherwise the whole records system was useless. The irony is, that if the bins had been in their former total confusion, the air commodore would have walked round placidly, and congratulated us on our hard work!

As I went to the door to close it after the visitors, I heard our officer say 'she has only very recently been promoted to corporal, and evidently hasn't got the hang of the work yet. We must put someone else in to take over.' This was too much! I seethed with rage, and muttered under my breath 'Judas! Beastly man! Horrible creature!' (There were not at that time the range of expletives for young ladies that are available now.) I went straight to the WAAF commanding officer and put in a request for a posting. You were supposed to give a reason for this, such as that you needed to be nearer to your invalid mother, who had just had a stroke. My reason was that it would be better if I were at a station where my languages could be useful to the war effort. The CO pointed out languidly that we all had qualifications which had in wartime to be temporarily abandoned for the greater good. I brought out my trump card: I said that the flying officer in charge did not find my work satisfactory. This was dangerous ground. There was no such thing then as a personality clash – or at least no language to describe it. Any WAAF who hinted at such a thing would have to be posted as far away as possible. The CO said that she would consult my boss, and would see what could be done to meet my request.

Chapter 3

David

ON A BLEAK DAY LATE in 1941 a young man stood on the windy railway platform at Cambridge. He was waiting for a train to take him to what he knew only as a rather seedy railway junction called Bletchley. The train he was waiting for was nicknamed the Cantab Crawler, and it was much beloved of dons wishing to spread out their manuscripts in empty carriages, because even in wartime it was so slow that very few people used it. It steamed gently out of Cambridge on a single line, halting at such bustling metropolises as Gamlingay and Potton, until it crept bashfully into Bletchley, where it was looked down upon by great bomb-scarred engines rushing north and south, full of troops and war materials. Meekly waiting until a line was clear, the little train puffed gallantly on to Oxford, where it rested for hours, until it was time for the arduous journey back to Cambridge.

The name of the young man waiting on the platform was David Wendt. Though outwardly impassive, he was in a ferment of mental excitement. He was in his second year at Trinity College and he had just been told by his tutor that his name had been given to an extremely hush-hush organisation at Bletchley which was looking for linguists. He was now on his way to an interview there.

He was not particularly excited to know that his destination was hush-hush, because 'hush-hush' was the current buzz word on the street. Everywhere was hush-hush. Advanced Flying Training Schools were terribly hush-hush, although the skies for miles around boomed and roared with strange antics. The Guard Dog Training School at Staverton was hush-hush, although enterprising locals brought boxes to stand on, so that they could look over the hedges at the day's exercises, and the dog handlers proudly brought their girlfriends to see them working. It was not the secret aspect of the Bletchley organisation that impressed David; it was the fact that they wanted linguists. Because what good was a foreign language unless you were in a place where that language was spoken? Even if he was not going to be trained as a spy, or parachuted into enemy-occupied country, translating Nazi documents was at least better than learning to form fours on some windy parade-ground.

David was, like most Englishmen, a scion of several races, with Scottish, German and Devonian blood in his veins. He had led the usual life of an upper-middle-class boy whose parents were in India, his father being in the Indian Civil Service. He spent holidays as well as term-time at his preparatory school at Bexhill; then at thirteen he went to public school at Tonbridge for five years, and then on to Cambridge. So far it had been an ordinary life for a boy like himself, but the outbreak of war in September 1939 changed everything. You could wait for the government to call you up, in which case you could be ordered wherever it wanted to send you; or you could volunteer for one of the Armed Services. In either case, you were no longer free to take charge of your own life.

When he arrived at the ugly junction of Bletchley, David looked at the instructions in his letter, and soon found himself at the great gates of Bletchley Park. While attempting to go through them, he was stopped by a guard, who asked for his pass and told him that no one – no one – could go through those gates without a pass. David showed him the letter inviting him to an interview, and was sent to a small wooden hut outside the gates. In it he found a room empty of everything but a table and two chairs. Sitting in one of the chairs was an immense man like a grizzly bear. He gave no sign of seeing his visitor. His eyes, overhung by heavy dark eyebrows, stared blankly ahead; his face was a huge landscape of crags and fissures, but it was a landscape utterly devoid of humanity. No sign of welcome or recognition appeared as David nervously spoke his own name, but when he laid his letter on the table a series of seismic waves and fissures broke across the face. It was like looking at a small earthquake. The great bulky figure leaped to its feet, knocking over its chair in the process, and seized David's hand in its huge paw. This was his first meeting with that great man and unsung genius J. E. S. Cooper, always known as Josh.

Josh had been recruited to Intelligence work in 1925 by Charles Morgan, then a distinguished but now a mostly over-looked novelist – Dylan Thomas would describe a boring conversation as being 'as long as half an hour with a novel by Charles Morgan'. The questions in the entrance exam had seemed so laughably simple to Josh that he thought there must be some catch somewhere which he was not clever enough to see; and being sure that he could not pass he did not trouble to finish the paper. Nevertheless, he got top marks. He worked with Ernst Fetterlein, who had been chief code-breaker to the tsar of all the Russias before the revolution, and whose son Paul was later to work in the German Air Section.

Josh now handed David a crumpled paper which consist-ed of a passage in German for translation and contained a number of words he had never seen before, since it appeared to be about some form of aerial direction-finding. David could make little of it. After a period of reflection, Josh asked in a kindly way about his interests and hobbies.

David had been a boy of passionate but very unusual in-terests. After leaving India at the age of five, he had found an Arabic grammar of his father's and, fascinated by the strange beauty of the language, had taught himself the Arabic alpha-bet. Later, during a school holiday, he had seen in the Brit-ish Museum a display of Persian miniatures and manuscripts, so he had bought a manual of Persian. At Cambridge he had learned to read an Urdu history of Arabian explorers. As a schoolboy his hobby had been making models of warships of different nations. Japanese destroyers had their names in kana on their sides, and he had taught himself the kana syllabary, memorising also the Japanese national anthem, written in characters plus kana. At this information Josh's face brightened, and he asked David to write down as much as he could remember of the anthem and the two syllabaries. David's successful performance of this task led to his being offered work at BP, as he was told to call Bletchley Park.

David was told nothing of the work he would be doing, only that everything to do with BP was 'Most Secret' – 'Top Secret' had not yet replaced the older and more dignified rubric. He would join the RAF, would rapidly be given the rank of sergeant and would probably later be commissioned to go overseas. Meanwhile he was to return to Cambridge and await instructions; and he was to let Josh know immediately if he received a call-up notice. He went back, happy to know that he was about to work for a man of such impressive personality.

Early in 1942 David was called up for the infantry. Josh, on being appealed to, told him to ignore the call-up papers and go at once to Cardington airfield, where he would enlist in the RAF as an AC2 in the trade of clerk/computor (a new one to puzzle the ladies in Records) – the word 'computer' having not yet been invented. At Cardington he was given no uniform but was told to go back to Cambridge on Deferred Service. Here, a few weeks later, he was summoned to an interview with the local recruiting officer, who appeared to think that he had been pulling strings to avoid military service. David, who had been warned never, under any circumstances, to mention BP, had virtually nothing to say in his own defence. But when the recruiting officer found out that David's father was Intelligence officer at Biggin Hill, he became less hostile.

This need for those working at the Park to keep absolute silence about their workplace could sometimes lead to comic or difficult situations. Gordon Welchman, one of the first men to help in the breaking of the Enigma ciphers, was called up for the Artillery when he was already doing secret work. The Foreign Office assured him that they would take care of this, but they did not, and he received a letter from the colonel of the unit he was supposed to report to. Again nothing was done, and finally he heard that the chief constable of Buckinghamshire had a warrant for his arrest. He wondered what would happen if he simply holed up in the Park, where not even a chief constable could get in without a pass.

But there were no army regulations for letting go of a man who had been called up but had not actually enlisted. After much haggling between the Foreign Office and army administration, it was decided that Welchman should report to a nearby Artillery unit and enlist, then be immediately discharged. He was enrolled by the sergeant in charge, a genial veteran of the First World War, and then, acutely conscious of the urgent work awaiting him at BP, asked for an instant discharge. The sergeant replied that this would not be possible, as a medical examination was required, and he himself was just going to lunch. Desperately Welchman found a local doctor who was just going to begin his lunch, and acquired the necessary medical certificates. Then he scoured local pubs until he found the sergeant and was at last discharged. The sergeant pressed into his hand as he left a leaflet urging him to join the Home Guard, where his army experience would be extremely useful. His army experience had actually lasted less than half an hour.

David completed his second-year tripos examinations, thus qualifying under wartime regulations for the degree of Bachelor of Arts. Meanwhile, some twenty young men had reported to the showroom of the Gas Company in Bedford for a course in Japanese. Josh had intended David to join them, but he had not completed his final exams. Had he been on this course, he would almost certainly have been sent abroad. By the time another course had been arranged, he was doing such useful work in a section dealing with Luftwaffe codes that Josh decided to keep him in his own German Air Section.

Chapter 4

The Interview

IN A REMARKABLY SHORT TIME the WAAF CO sent me a chit requiring me to report for interview to the Air Ministry in Holborn. I thought gleefully that this must be for a posting where my languages might be used, although I was sorry to leave our little band of sisters who were working so hard to get the record cards in some sort of order. But I was also still feeling bitter about my betrayal (as I saw it) by the officer in charge of our room, and being very young and vindictive I thought I would never be able to work with him again. In fact he had not visited our room since the incident of the Important Visitor.

I went on trying to empty the big bin of its misfiled cards, but all the fun had gone out of it, because I saw that unless we WAAFs went on continually working like this (which we could not do) all the bins would quite quickly slide back into the muddle they had been in before our crusade to clean them up. And I am sure that they did, though I never heard from RAF Records after I had left. When I thought of the dear ladies and their bins, I used to say to myself, with Othello, 'Chaos is come again.'

I was not really supposed to leave until after lunch, but I had been given my travel warrant so I slipped into Gloucester on an early transport. I was not going to miss the chance of a day in London. I sat in the train watching the exquisitely beautiful English countryside glide by. The water meadows just outside Gloucester (now drained and housing big garage installations) were full of kingcups; other fields shone with buttercups and daisies. The roads were empty but for an occasional convoy of army lorries or a despatch rider speeding past. Lovely little villages with thatched cottages, probably quite insanitary but covered with clematis and wisteria, ought to have been hymned by a poet. Suburban gardens had all been dug up and filled with vegetables, but lilac and laburnum still bloomed, and red and white may blossomed everywhere. Even bombed London had on its springtime dress of chickweed, speedwell and scarlet pimpernel, where in autumn ragged robin and rosebay-willowherb would cover all the ruined sites.

I thought about what I would do in London. I would go to a photographer to show my mother my corporal's stripes. I would walk down Regent Street, where (so the rumour went) there was a shop where you could buy underclothes without coupons, because they were made of captured German parachute silk. We in the Services had no clothing coupons because all our clothes were supplied, but the dark blue winter knickers and the light blue summer ones (called 'midnights' and 'twilights' by airmen privileged to catch sight of them) did not at all resemble camiknickers made of silk, even if the silk was made in Germany. Then I would go to a lunchtime concert at the National Gallery, and have lunch at a British Restaurant, where for one shilling and sixpence you could have soup and main course or main course and sweet. Then, for the high spot of my visit, I would stroll down Charing Cross Road, looking into all the second-hand bookshops until the interview, which was at half past four.

I did all this, and by the time I had squeezed through the sand-bagged entrance to the Air Ministry I was beginning to think I had done too much, for I had quite a bad headache. I was shown into a stuffy small room on an upper floor, which contained nothing but a bench and an inner door, from which came the sound of voices. I longed for a drink of water, but dared not leave the room. The door opened and a young air-man came out. 'What a bastard,' he mouthed silently, then said aloud, 'you're to go in now.' By this time a series of small hammers was banging on my forehead from inside my head. I had taken my hat off, and now left it on the bench – a deadly crime – as I went into the interview room.

The inner room was no more lavishly furnished than the waiting room, just a wooden table and two chairs, in one of which sat a bored-looking wing commander. He told me to sit down and handed me a printed sheet, which I was supposed to translate. I bent my aching eyes on it and could see immedi-ately that it was an article about some new research in aircraft control and was full of technical terms. I handed it back and said, in German, that I could make very little of it. He replied that I must try, but after I had stumbled through a few paragraphs he said sharply that we were wasting each other's time, and that my vocabulary was insufficient for the purposes for which I should be needed. For some reason, this infuriated me, even though it was perfectly true. 'I bet my vocabulary is better than yours,' I said angrily against the pounding of my head. I felt very very hot indeed. 'Have you read as much Schiller and Goethe as I have? Do you know a lot of the *Dichterliebe* by heart? How many German songs can you sing?'

Suddenly a dreadful premonition overcame me. 'Oh God', I said, sinking my head on the table, 'I think I'm going to be sick.' The wing commander acted with commendable promptitude. With his foot he slid a metal waste-paper basket towards me, and loudly rang a bell on his table. This brought a sergeant, who was told to take me to a washroom, where I was very sick, and then, pale and shuddering, I was taken back to the wing commander. The sergeant was told to get a car and take me to Paddington, where he would not leave until he had seen me on the Gloucester train. 'And see that she has her hat and haversack,' he added. As I stumbled out I thought I heard him say 'I don't go in for poetry much myself.' He sounded as though he were laughing.

I remember hardly anything of the train journey, and when I reached Gloucester I had only one thought in my mind. This was to get to the WAAF sick quarters in the Bell Hotel, which was not far away. I banged on the door until it was opened, when I slid forward and laid my burning cheek on the cool linoleum. It felt lovely, and I wanted to stay there for ever, but some time later I found myself in bed, with a WAAF orderly offering me a glass of water and two tablets. 'You're in for it,' she said sympathetically, 'they sent a transport to the station for you – somebody rang up from the Air Ministry, I believe – and when you didn't turn up they marked you AWOL. You'd be better off dead.'

I thought so too. The tablets I had taken were the dreaded M & B, the Services' answer, in those pre-antibiotic days, to everything except broken limbs and childbirth. They seemed to be a powerful kind of drench, though never used by the Veterinary Corps because animals were too valuable to be subjected to such a drastic remedy. They made you feel dreadfully, appallingly ill. Presumably they made all germs feel the same, since after about three days all symptoms had disappeared; or, if they had not, you still felt much better than you had felt while taking the tablets.

So on the fourth day after my arrival at the Bell, feeling limp and washed out, I went back to my station, there to face the wrath of the WAAF commanding officer. Because I really had been ill, I was not put on a charge, but all my crimes were laid out before me at great length: I had not waited for the transport; I had not sent a message back to camp; I had not waited to ask permission to go on Sick Parade but had gone straight to sick quarters. This really was a parade. The wheezing, limping, giddy wretches who had been given permission to consult the MO (medical officer) were actually brought to attention by a sergeant, marched across the parade ground to the MO's office and stood at ease in tempest, blizzard or blazing sun until a yawning orderly admitted them. Fainting or vomiting on the way was regarded with disapproval as 'conduct unbefitting'.

I was rather chastened by the CO's tirade, but was brought up short when at the end of it she said sharply that she hoped I should behave better at my next station. 'Because', she said, 'you are posted to Chicksands with effect from Saturday.' I was amazed; my interview had assumed a dreamlike quality in my mind. I thought vaguely that I had been tried for some translating job and found wanting. I rushed into the Records Office and found the bin for Chicksands. It appeared, from the number of wireless operators stationed there, to be some kind of wireless station; it had to be more interesting than Records anyhow. I had no hope that my record card would find its way into the correct bin, and indeed it didn't, but not, remarkably enough, through misfiling but for quite another reason.

Being posted involved visits to every department of the camp. It was like moving house but more laborious and time-consuming. It was quite restful to sit at last in the train on the way to Bedford, and rather exciting to be swooped to Chicksands in the sidecar of an RAF motorbike. It was, however, disconcerting when I went into the admin. office to report my arrival, to be told, 'Don't put your kit down, corporal. You're going on right away.' Where was I going on, and why? I realised what was happening when the sergeant said to a driver, who was lounging about the office, 'now, are you going to blindfold her, or take her in the covered van?' The regulars were always playing jokes on the young WAAFs, and it was best to go along with them and pretend to laugh afterwards. 'Well, the van's ready,' said the driver, and picked up my kitbag and haversack. I sat in the back of the van, separated from the driver by a sheet of hardboard and with the windows blacked out. The drive went on an awfully long time for a joke, and it occurred to me that, since the sergeant at Chicksands had not booked me in, the last documentary evidence of my journey was my travel warrant which had been collected by the railway transport officer at Bedford. At last, however, the van stopped, the doors opened and my kit and I were swiftly ejected. Before I could ask the driver where I was, he was back in the van, had made a U-turn and sped off.

There were a pair of rather magnificent gates before me, but they were closed. A smaller gate was open at one side, with a guardhouse and a guard standing near. I went up to him and showed him my papers. 'Can't come in here,' he said without looking at them, 'got no pass.' I was by this time hungry, thirsty and very, very annoyed. 'Look,' I said, 'I don't know where I am, and I don't know what I'm supposed to do.' 'Come to the right place, then,' said the guard, 'the most on 'em here look as if they didn't know where they was, and God knows what they'm doing.'

An elderly guard told him to leave me alone, and said that I was to go to the hut at the left of the gates (the hut where, unknown to me, David had been interviewed). 'Somebody will come and see to you,' he said, 'and if you want to know where you are, you're at Bletchley Park.' 'And if you want to know what that is,' added the younger guard, sniggering, 'it's the biggest lunatic asylum in Britain.'

Chapter 5

Talk about the Park

IT HAS ALWAYS GIVEN ME great pleasure to remember that a house built by a Jew, who brought up his Jewish family there and doubtless entertained many Jewish friends, should have been instrumental in defeating Adolf Hitler, that great oppressor and murderer of the Jewish race.

The Bletchley Park estate actually appears in the *Domesday Book*, and in 1882 it was bought by Herbert Leon, who was later created baronet. He had lavish ideas, and his house was built in the grand style. It is always described in books as 'an ugly redbrick mansion' and as 'a curious mixture of mock-Tudor and Gothic' by the early code-breakers, who all seem to have thought it hideous. Robert Harris, who did not see it in wartime, seems to have hated it. In *Enigma* he calls it 'a nightmare . . . the styles sulked and raged against one another.'

But I loved the house and longed to explore it. It reminded me of one of those American Christmas cakes, which instead of icing are stuck all over with pecans, brazils, walnuts and glacé cherries. In fact, the house was stuck all over with gables, arcades, belvederes, tourelles, a small tower and even a green copper dome; it was delicious. The estate must have been glorious too, with rose gardens, a lake, tennis courts, a cobbled stable yard and even a ha-ha, from which guests could survey the flat Buckinghamshire countryside. There was a rumour that there had been a baby maze, too.

But when it was bought by the government in the days before the war, armies of workmen took it over. A high fence was built all round the park, which in early days was guarded by men of the RAF regiment, whose sergeant was one day heard saying to a delinquent, 'If you don't pull your socks up, you'll be sent inside.' It would seem that the idea of BP as a home for psychiatric patients was early established.

When electric cables, telephone and teleprinter lines had been laid, the workmen began to build huts. It may be expedient here to destroy the fiction, created by the television programme, that BP was mysteriously named 'Station X', to preserve its anonymity. In fact, the tower was for a very short time made into a wireless room, which was named Station X because it was the tenth of a number of wireless units which used Roman numerals, to distinguish them from other units which used Arabic numbers. When the station moved to Whaddon, the name went too.

When all lines, drains and cables were laid, the workmen began to build huts on the ground where the maze, the rose garden and the ha-ha had been. The tennis courts, the stables and the lake remained. The lake was really a large pond, in which swam some rather indeterminate fish, a colony of frogs and a few ducks. Ducks are very poor mothers, and strollers round the lake in springtime found it wise to avert their eyes from ducklings in distress.

The huts were made of Canadian pine, and were freezingly cold in winter and stuffy in summer. Some had tortoise stoves, while others boasted oil stoves which either burnt fiercely for a short time or smouldered without warmth. Some of the later huts contained radiators, which gave out a faint heat, leading chilly code-breakers to huddle against them, trying to get their mittened fingers warm enough to continue their work.

All the huts were renumbered so often that no one who worked in one can agree as to what its number was. Only Huts Six and Three, which one worker in Hut Six called 'the code-breakers' Bethlehem', retained their original hut numbers even when they moved into D Block. In Hut Six the Enigma messages were read, and in Hut Three the material was evaluated. As papers were continually passed from hut to hut, a wonderful piece of modern technology was constructed to simplify this. A small wooden tunnel was made between the huts. A box with a string at each end was kept in it, and when it was full of papers someone in Hut Six knocked on the wood with a ruler, upon which anyone who heard the knocking would pull the box by its string through the tunnel to Hut Three, where the papers were taken out. Any papers to go back were then loaded, and this highly complex procedure repeated from the other end. The people in Hut Six who translated the decrypts had little idea of the importance of the material they were dealing with. They merely wrote down the translations, which were then taken away to be evaluated.

We lowlier code-breakers saw the people from these huts walking about the Park, in the corridors, in the canteen or in the clubhouse. We recognised their faces sometimes, but we had no idea what their work was. It was only long after the war that we read about Enigma and Ultra, and realised that these were the 'pundits' – the 'enwised'. (Remarkably enough, as one of the Hut Six workers pointed out, 'you never discussed your work with anyone except your little group that you worked with. I hadn't a clue what was going on in the rest of the Park and nobody else had a clue what we were doing, except the real high-ups. It was a curious world of its own.')

A bizarre group of people worked in these two huts that were so vital to the war: Alan Turing (who often stayed in the hut at night to do his own research), Gordon Welchman (a brilliant mathematician), Jim Rose (who was involved with inaugurating the Penguin Group), Peter Calvocoressi, Hugh Alexander (the British chess champion, who had taught mathematics at Winchester College) and Oliver Strachey (Lytton's brother). Then there were F. L. Lucas (author of *The Decline and Fall of the Romantic Ideal* and a kind of guru to the younger ones) and Harry Hinsley (one of the few code-breakers not from the upper classes but from a working-class home in the Black Country, and who was destined to become one of the most brilliant Bletchleyites and to achieve academic eminence). Stuart Milner-Barry (who had won the British boys' chess championship in 1923) was there, as were the German-born

Ettinghausen brothers and the Penderel twins (who were under eighteen years old and so were entitled to supplies of NAMCO, a government-allocated milk cocoa powder, which they kindly shared with others on their shift). Somewhere about the Park roamed Angus Wilson (who was indisputably camp, though the word was not then known to the general public), A. J. Alan (famous broadcaster of short stories), Peter Benenson (later to found Amnesty International), the young Roy Jenkins and a Muslim with a Scottish accent. There was also a naval Lieutenant Commander Tandy, who had a degree in forestry, and when asked at his interview if he had any special interest modestly replied that he was knowledgeable about cryptogams (small aquatic flora). His interviewer, either mishearing or misunderstanding, at once recommended him for BP, where he soon became expert in cryptograms too.

Those who actually broke the Enigma and Fish codes have had a great deal of publicity and praise, and rightly so. Without their work, Great Britain might have been starved into submission by the Nazis; at the very least, the war would have lasted much longer. But even they, as well as the humblest code-breakers, depended entirely on another set of people – the wireless operators. Without the messages they intercepted, there would have been little to decode. Bletchley Park was at the centre of a network of intercept sites, run by the army, the navy, the RAF, the Foreign Office, the Post Office and, surprisingly, the Metropolitan Police. In fact one of the most important sites for the interception of German Air traffic was the police station at Denmark Hill in London!

Monitoring German traffic was one of the most demanding jobs of the war. A radio operator had first to do an intensive six-month course. Then, after further training, he or she had to take another intensive course in the care and maintenance of radio equipment. When posted, eight-hour shifts were the normal working pattern, and while on shift you dared not relax for a second. Your airwaves might be silent, but at any moment transmission might begin, and it was imperative that you catch especially the preamble and the first groups, because these told you who was sending to whom, and could hold the key to the whole message. If the weather or the sending was poor, or the transmitter distant, single letters or whole groups might be missed, but these blanks and garbles had to be logged as carefully as the rest of the transmission. Very weak signals from outstations were difficult to pick up, as were transmissions from the Russian front. If a particular frequency was very important, it would be monitored by two operators at different stations, and the results 'melded', in the hope that groups missed by one operator might have been picked up by the other. If traffic was heavy, an operator could come off duty wringing cramped fingers and with ears buzzing.

And then there were the transport workers, both drivers and mechanics. If you were billeted in or near Bletchley, you could walk or cycle to work. One of the code-breakers in the film *Enigma* was able to borrow a car with a tank capacity of about ten gallons and drive all the way to Scotland without any petrol coupons, but few of us had such accommodating friends, so we used the transport to bring us in from our outlying villages. The transport was a job lot of vehicles ranging from very old buses through out-of-date army trucks to shooting brakes and even small seaside charabancs. The trouble was, as usual, that Bletchley Park did not exist, so Edward Green, the equipment manager, could not indent in the ordinary way for a fleet of modern buses. He had to collect piecemeal whatever he could from wherever he could, and for his efforts he became known as 'Scrounger'. But the drivers were always reliable and always turned up on time, and the mechanics somehow kept these old crocks on the road, snatching when they could a few hours' sleep in the former maids' rooms, which were at the top of the mansion.

Your transport picked you up at a set point, but if you weren't there on time it couldn't wait; it had, on arrival at the Park, to take home the weary workers from the preceding shift. There were three shifts: eight till four, four till midnight and midnight till eight the next morning. Coming on to the midnight shift was the most eerie time. The incoming bus would draw up on the left of the grass circle in front of the mansion. As you climbed out, yawning already at the prospect of the long night before you, you were aware of dimly seen groups of silent people waiting on the other side of the circle, who, in the cloudy dark or pale moonlight or mists of rain, were like spirits waiting for Charon to ferry them across the Styx.

The drivers had none of the cheerful chatter and joking that other transport drivers had; the journeys were for the most part silent. I suppose that convoys of WRNS or teleprinter girls who were all billeted together in some stately home might sing or gossip as they travelled, but, whether by accident or design, most people were billeted in places where the other passengers were strangers. In other wartime stations you talked about your boss, your workmates, comic incidents at work or small mishaps, but in BP all such talk was taboo. The need-to-know principle was paramount. You knew the people who worked in your own section, though if it was a large section, occupying more than one room, you might know only the people in the room you worked in. A girl who had been at BP almost from the beginning told me that, if there were an invasion, each of us would be able only to give the Nazis an insignificant shred of information. All the pundits, all those who knew anything of importance, would have been on their way to Canada.

And last, but never least, were the landladies. Until the army and Air Force camps were built, there would have simply been no room for all the workers at BP unless a great crowd of women had offered to lodge us in their homes, often with real warmth and friendliness. Doubtless they were glad to have an extra ration book, because the code-breakers ate at least one meal six days a week in the canteen, and were often away on their day's leave too. But they were paid a pittance, and they had to put up with people leaving before midnight, coming back after midnight, leaving before eight in the morning and requiring quiet for sleep after the night shift. No 'perks' could be brought back from their workplace, and no gossip to enthral the neighbours. Almost certainly they had been told by the billeting officer that in no circumstances were they to attempt to find out where their lodger worked or what he or she did; and indeed I never heard of one landlady who did. Nor did I ever hear of any landlady in the least like Robert Harris's Mrs Ethel Armstrong in *Enigma*, who was grasping, inquisitive and strict. The ones I heard of (though accents and habits must often have been strange to them) put heavy stone hotwater bottles in beds on cold nights, left kettles on the hob for lodgers coming in at midnight, did not complain if two of them were on different shifts, or kept a slice of Christmas pudding for workers not granted Christmas leave. I hope Heaven is as kind to them as they were to us.

Then there were the despatch riders, who rode at speed through blazing sun, blackest night, torrential rain, blizzards or roads heaped with snow to bring pouches and bags of intercepts and other documents to Bletchley. I heard of three who were killed in this arduous and dangerous work. And we should not forget the intercept sites, where it was absolutely vital that, no matter what catastrophe took place, traffic was never left unmonitored. There was a Special Wireless Section, which monitored German Army traffic in the area of the beachheads after D-Day (6 June 1944). The section's camp was set up in a field in Bishop's Waltham. A house nearby was occupied by the ATS Signals Section, which provided a teleprinter link to Bletchley Park. One evening later that month, just at dusk, a 'buzz-bomb' – as the V1 missiles were called – was shot down over the camp and exploded into it, leaving a huge crater and wounding seventeen men, some very seriously. While these were taken to hospital, immediate replacements were arranged, most of them from men who had not long come off shift; and the watch went on as usual after a matter of minutes. Those who kept BP supplied with traffic all round the clock have never had the recognition they deserve.

And if you saw *Band of Brothers*, it was from intercepts by the Special Wireless Section that BP could give the early warning which enabled the American Easy Company to repel on 12 June 1944 the German counterattack on Carentan and hold the town.

Chapter 6

German Air Section

A CODE CONSISTS OF GROUPS of symbols used to represent letters, numerals, words or phrases in common use. A cipher is any method of transforming a given text to conceal its meaning. So that although books, TV programmes and films refer to 'decoding' Enigma messages, the Enigma machines were in themselves merely enciphering and deciphering implements. They could not even print out the messages sent and received by their means. They were of course fiendishly complicated machines, since the rotors (though not on the naval three-rotor machine) could be permuted in sixty different ways; the three wheels could be set initially in 17,576 diverse ways. The plugboard could go through 150 million million circuit changes, so that altogether there were 158 million million million possible settings for every message. Even if you could afford to employ a million million million people to decode each message, it might be 159 days before one of them was successful, by which time the information contained in it would be out of date and therefore useless. The Germans thought that, if used properly, its ciphers would be unbreakable.

The basic Enigma machine had been invented in 1919 by a Dutchman, who had hawked it round all the Foreign Offices in Europe. They all turned it down. The only country to purchase it was Germany, then bankrupt and devastated by its defeat in World War One and the demands of the Versailles Treaty. Possibly its leaders were already thinking of reclaiming their lost territories and their national prestige. Their navy first used it in 1926, the army took it up two years later (adding a plugboard which greatly improved its security) and the German Air Force in the middle thirties. It was also used by the Intelligence and security forces and other important government departments.

Hitler's High Command was convinced that messages sent by properly trained Enigma operators should be impregnable to an enemy. All their most secret messages could, they thought, be transmitted in perfect safety, impossible for any unauthorised person to decode. He and his generals derived immense confidence from the conviction that their plans to annex Sudetenland, Czechoslovakia and Poland were hidden from all eyes by their unbreakable cipher. Every German regiment or division, and every corps commander in the field, was accompanied by a specially equipped control vehicle containing an Enigma machine with its operators. Pretty well all other organisations sent at least their top-grade messages through Enigma. Hitler often communicated with his generals and high officials by this means, as did the Abwehrdienst and the

Sicherheitsdienst (the Secret Intelligence Service of the High Command). Tactical and operational orders for all Services were delivered through Enigma.

The machine looked like an old-fashioned typewriter, with circular keys on short thick stalks, each key marked with a letter of the alphabet. You should dismiss from your mind the image of fingers swiftly tapping out vital messages, to be speedily received – that was not how Enigma worked. Each heavy key had to be pressed down hard with a single finger, when a different letter lit up on the lampboard, which was placed directly above the keyboard and which consisted of twenty-six small circular windows with a tiny electric bulb behind each. The keyboard operator did the pressing of keys, while the cipher clerk sat close to him and read out each letter of the original message to him. It was also this man's job to write down the enciphered letter when it appeared in its own little lit-up circle. When complete, the message, which consisted of the letters which the cipher clerk had written down, was given to a third clerk, who took it to a wireless operator to be transmitted in Morse code to its recipient. It was a laborious performance, but then complete confidentiality was worth a lot of work. Wasn't it?

But before this complicated procedure could even be initiated, the operator had to perform even more complicated actions. He had first to consult the current page of the Enigma key list (changed every month), specifying which three out of a box of five wheels, called rotors, must be selected for the day in question, and in which order they must be locked on to the machine. This function was called the *Walzenlage*. Then, consulting the key list again, the operator had to take from another box some double-ended rubber-covered leads (usually twenty) and plug each end as prescribed into twenty of the twenty-six sockets of the plugboard (*Steckerbrett*). He had to leave six sockets empty, and plug each lead exactly as he was told, because plugging 'A' into 'M' instead of 'N' would garble the whole message. Finally, he had to turn his three rotors to an absolutely random three-letter setting. This sounds the simplest of all the procedures, but in fact it was often the most difficult. No portable wartime machine could produce completely random sequences, or not for very long, and nor apparently can the human mind. The Enigma operator was very likely to key in three letters that resonated in some way in his mind: his girlfriend's initials, the first three letters of a rude word, or the German equivalents of BBC, ITV, NHS or some similar acronym. This could be of great help to the codebreakers, as was the fact that no letter could be enciphered as itself. If the 'A' key was pressed, the only letter that could never come up in the lampboard was 'A'. Another great weakness was that Enigma was reciprocal: if 'A' enciphered as 'C', then at the same setting 'C' enciphered as 'A'.

That super-intelligent tactician Admiral Doenitz, commander of Hitler's U-boats, was, as far as we know, the only one of the High Command who had a suspicion that Enigma was being broken, which it was. All the other influential Germans rubbished his idea, although the Germans did make some improvements to Enigma and its procedures from mid-

1943 onwards. When Doenitz issued a more comprehensive code book, Bletchley lost its key into the code they called Shark, which was used by the U-boats in the Atlantic for communicating with their base. He also ordered the Atlantic U-boats to start using a more complex Enigma machine, with a fourth rotor, for all messages. This completely blocked Bletchley's access to the Atlantic U-boat traffic, and hundreds of thousands of tons of merchant shipping were sunk every month.

The code-breakers in Hut Eight found their way back into Shark on 13 December 1942, and Ultra helped convoys to avoid the U-boats or provided information showing which convoys were about to be attacked. In late May 1943 Doenitz called off his 'wolf packs', and after that the U-boats were never so successful again.

There were various types of Enigma machines, including naval Enigma (with which we are not concerned here) and the standard German army and air force machine (which, apart from modifications introduced in 1944, was exactly the same as the naval three-rotor model). The lightest Enigma machine weighed fourteen pounds, and the most commonly used one was some twenty-eight pounds. Each machine had to be stabilised on a fixed bench or table.

It is easy to see that there were many situations in which it would be impossible to send messages by Enigma. It would, for instance, be quite ludicrous to imagine its complicated manoeuvres going on in a bomber plane during a raid, or in a fighter plane in an aerial battle. How, then, were air-to-ground or ground-to-air messages transmitted or received?

The answer to that question is the reason why the German Air Section was founded and organised by Josh Cooper. The very few authors who even refer to the contribution to the war effort made by the decoding of Luftwaffe traffic tend to dismiss this as insignificant, probably because they know little or nothing of the work done by this section.

Short-range aircraft such as fighters, dive-bombers or light liaison planes carried no wireless operator, and used only VHF (Very High Frequency) voice for the pilot to communicate with base or with other pilots. (VHF was restricted to line-of-sight range.) Fighter pilots had neither time nor attention to spare for elaborate codes. Both British and German pilots used only simple cover terms such as 'angels' for altitude and 'bandits' (the actual term the Germans used was 'Indianer') for hostile aircraft. Bombers and transport planes used RT (Radio Telegraphy) when close to base and for communications among themselves, but to keep in touch with base during long flights, from hostile territory or far out to sea, they had to use HF WT (High Frequency Morse), and their messages were sent in low-grade code. To supplement the highly secret radar sites, at the outbreak of war the RAF set up listening posts along the south and east coasts, manned chiefly by WAAFs with a good knowledge of German, to monitor all RT.

The Germans were convinced that Enigma offered good security for their high-level communications between the supreme commands and regional commands. (Gordon Welchman agreed that Enigma would have been impregnable if properly used.) For the more routine administrative traffic between the regions, they relied on other systems. For cases where a few hours' security was considered adequate, the Luftwaffe employed a variety of small code books usually enciphered by simple substitution, with changes at intervals of the key sheets used to recipher the original three-letter groups. Chief among the codes which David Wendt and I would encounter in our work in the German Air Section was the AuKa-Tafel (Aufklaerungs und Kampfflieger Signalstafel Land und See), meaning reconnaissance and bomber code. This was a small booklet of about a dozen pages; in different sections were the letters of the alphabet, figures zero to ten, zero–zero, eleven to ninety-nine, hundreds and thousands, aircraft both German and Allied, ship types, weather terms and general vocabulary. Opposite each item was a three-figure number, running in sequence from 001 upwards. There were also blanks in the code book opposite some numbers, so that the user unit could insert special words or phrases useful to them. They could insert place names or the names of objects associated with their special sphere of operations, which might be Russia, North Africa or Norway. These blank groups were called *Verfuegungssignale* (groups for use as desired). In BP-speak they were 'Verfugs'.

These basic three-figure code groups were then reciphered into three-letter groups which were listed in a key sheet accompanying the code book. The key sheet had two parts: encipher, which listed in numerical sequence the three-figure numbers of the code, each opposite a random three-letter group; and decipher, which of course listed the letter groups in alphabetical order opposite their equivalent three-figure group.

For example, an encoder wishing to send the message '*Heute keine Sendung*' (no transmission today) would look up in his code book the three-figure groups for his three words, which might be 102 168 242. He would then turn to his key sheets for the current month and look up those groups, opposite which would appear the three-letter groups – say, JBG AZN BBZ. These groups made up the message to be sent in Morse. As the month went on, many frequently used groups would become so familiar that there was no need to look them up. If the sender wished to include a word not appearing in the code book he would spell it out, using the groups for letters of the alphabet. These 'spellers' were usually the easiest messages for the code-breakers to decode, and would often provide other useful 'kracks'. The actual AuKa code books rarely changed; however, the key sheets changed initially at midnight on the last day of each month, and later on a daily basis.

These books contained about two hundred groups, so that only a small number of the thousands of possible three-letter combinations were ever used. To avoid confusion with the Q-code (a code consisting of three-letter groups each beginning with the letter 'Q', introduced in 1909 to facilitate communication between maritime radio operators speaking different languages), no code book ever used any groups beginning with 'Q'. But, naturally enough, the compilers of the key sheets used letter groups which could most easily, quickly and recognisably be transmitted in Morse. So one set of cipher sheets had groups AAC, AAG, AAH, AAK, while AAA, AAB and AAD were not used. The preferences of individual departments or special peculiarities made good recognition features for our intercept operators.

WT traffic from bombers was extremely terse, as the Germans well knew that long transmissions gave opportunities for D/F (Direction Finding) to locate the transmitter; so bomber crews were instructed to keep their messages to a bare minimum. Only when the bombers came west after smashing Poland were the British able to hear their codes. An RAF squadron leader was able with his flying experience to break into them, greatly aided by the code books captured from German aircraft shot down in France and during the Battle of Britain, in 1940.

Josh Cooper saw that these low-grade codes should be investigated, because they might contribute in some as yet unforeseen ways to the overall picture of the German Air Force. Doubtless he had to fight to get funding and manpower, but at some time in 1940 a handful of RAF men and women, with a few civilians, began work huddled in a corner of the library in the mansion. As the work expanded, so did the workforce, and they were given a few rooms in one of the wooden huts. By the end of 1943 a much-enlarged section was transferred to two spurs in F Block, in the north-west corner of the Park.

The reasons for creating the German Air Section now seem incontrovertible. The British had to check at least some of the low-grade Luftwaffe material, since there was always the chance that some scrap of vital information would turn up, and it seemed more cost-effective in the long run to maintain continuous cover than sample it at intervals only to find that our analysts could no longer pick up where they had left off without time-wasting and troublesome reworking. Many details trivial in themselves provided the Air Ministry with a clear picture of the Luftwaffe's equipment, capabilities and order of battle, and these details could be combined with the quite different kind of information obtained from high-grade ciphers. Summaries from German Air helped the experts to assess the degree to which losses in action, fuel shortages and decline in numbers of fully trained aircrew affected combat readiness and morale. (RAF Intelligence often wildly overestimated numbers of German planes shot down or destroyed. BP was able to make estimates much closer to the reality.)

In *Station X* Michael Smith points out that the interception of low-level communications provided vital tactical evidence on the preparations of German bombers and their fighter escorts. BP gave advance notice of the planned times of raids, intended targets and the numbers of aircraft involved. Unfortunately these were subject – for weather and other reasons – to sudden and unannounced changes, so that this information was often disregarded by the Air Ministry. Sometimes Enigma messages repeated in AuKa code to a station not possessing an Enigma machine would provide a vital clue to Hut Six (and sometimes Hut Eight), by giving an entry to their current keys.

But whatever the reasons for monitoring the low-level codes during the period when the threat of a German invasion was real, it was necessary to glean every scrap of information about enemy air power, since desperate air battles and raids on airfields were of daily occurrence.

Gradually, of course, the Luftwaffe declined from being an immediate deadly threat in 1940 to virtual impotence in 1945. This led to the abandonment of many lines of work, to decreasing numbers of people in the section and the turning of the remaining personnel to Japanese codes.

When it had been small and insignificant, none of the authorities cared much what happened to it. Later, as it grew in size and importance, there were power struggles and takeover attempts behind the scenes. At first it was under Air Ministry control and had an RAF Orderly Room for administration; later it passed into the hands of the Foreign Office. It mattered little to us who our nominal masters were; we owed allegiance only to Josh Cooper.

Chapter 7

David Gets to Work

BEFORE DAVID WENDT and I arrived at Bletchley Park in the spring and early summer of 1942, a great deal had happened in the war and at BP itself. From May until August 1940, Britain had lived under the threat of invasion by Hitler's troops, and a certain number of people from BP were chosen to go abroad to safety, since it would have been essential to go on reading the German codes from afar if the country were ever to be freed. I suppose, but I don't know, that as far as possible unmarried men were picked, since it would certainly have been impossible for families to accompany them. They were given passports and special identification and were told to keep a suitcase always packed, ready to depart at a moment's notice. All other workers were ordered to disperse to distant homes or relatives as soon as invasion was announced. As usual, the Park could not identify itself for supplies, because it did not officially exist, so a fleet of dilapidated old buses was commandeered to take the fugitives to Liverpool, but one of the organisers had great doubts whether the column would get further than a few miles.

Although fortunately Hitler thought better of his proposed invasion, the non-existence of BP was often a problem – not only in the matter of supplies. Only a very few, very senior officers had been informed about it. Hut Three could usually get information to the War Office and the Air Ministry, though they had to go through MI6 (the espionage department). Any naval intelligence, usually of the utmost importance needing immediate action, had to go through the Admiralty's OIC (Operational Intelligence Centre), whose personnel often showed little interest in the information.

Harry Hinsley reported a great deal of German naval activity in the Baltic, which was completely ignored by the OIC, so that the British were taken by surprise when Norway was invaded. Again, they ignored his reports about the sailing of the *Scharnhorst* and the *Gneisenau*, which led to the sinking of the aircraft carrier HMS *Glorious* and her two accompanying destroyers. For a fortnight before, Hinsley had telephoned the OIC twice a day, begging them to inform the fleet, but, as he himself said, 'the OIC . . . resisted Bletchley's suggestion that such a warning should be sent to ships at sea. It was not prepared to accept inferences drawn from an untried technique by civilians as yet unknown to its staff.'

Although attempts were made to form a better relationship, they were not very successful. Charles Morgan, who worked in naval intelligence, thought that there was a great deal of professional jealousy – that rather than call BP, the OIC preferred to use its own information, however incomplete. Hinsley thought it was purely personal, that the OIC was angry that BP had better sources than their own, and was determined to be obstructive. This kind of opposition was quite foreign to BP, whose code-breakers always applauded any breakthrough by one of their members, and who lived in a happy atmosphere of support and enthusiasm.

But enthusiasm and helpfulness cannot take the place of practical resources. BP simply had not enough of anything, from code-breakers, intercept sets, bombes (electrical machines with rotating drums equating to the rotors of Enigma machines) and their operators to pencils and paper. Therefore on 21 October 1941 Gordon Welchman, Alan Turing, Stuart Milner-Barry and Hugh Alexander wrote a letter to Winston Churchill himself, and Milner-Barry went in person to 10 Downing Street to deliver it, which after great difficulties he did. Churchill responded with his famous minute to his chief-of-staff, 'Make sure they have all they want; extreme priority and report to me this has been done.' He scrawled across the minute 'action this day.' After that, resources began to flow into the Park. I have sometimes thought that my posting there, after that disastrous interview, was because of the need to get three thousand more people into BP at top speed.

The pundits presumably had some idea, even if a very slight one, of the kind of work they would be doing at BP; some of them had been on various kinds of training course. But the rank and file, on the whole, had none. The general practice was the old apprentice ploy: you sat next to someone who was doing what you would later do, and by watching him (and from his explanations if he was helpful, which most people were) you learned enough to strike out on your own.

David Wendt was fortunate: he had been put into a room with a cheerful young civilian who was leaving to have a baby, and before she left she showed him exactly what to do and explained why it needed to be done. He was given a set of sheets listing three-letter groups and their meanings, as recovered by the midnight-to-eight shift at Cheadle, and a supply of large sheets of paper ruled in printed columns and rows, as well as a stack of forms containing the messages taken up to then. His job was to copy in time order these messages, one under the other, starting in the left margin with details of time of intercept, to/from and preamble. Such a compilation of messages using the same code was known as a 'depth'. Next, David was to insert on the blank line below the message text the meanings from the recovery sheet. There were naturally blanks where the meaning was unknown. In due course, when he had gained experience and confidence, he was encouraged to suggest meanings of his own; and also to teach himself Morse with a view to amending possible blanks or garbles, whether errors by the sender or by the intercept operator, contending with atmospherics, fading and fatigue.

David discovered that a single dot more or less could change an 'S' to an 'H' or a 'B' to an 'N'. At the end of the day we signalled all our recoveries to interested parties under the title 'Rhino posses', a name derived from the group RHN, from which we recognised this code because the group RHN was

to be found in its recipher tables. The messages came in overnight from the intercept sites in bundles of very cheap paper
with lines of teleprinter tape stuck on. Some of the groups had
already been deciphered by the midnight-to-eight shift. Our
intercept operators could often use as an aid to identification
a feature known as 'good groups'. David (with his massive
brain and perfect memory still extant in his eighties) kindly
explained to me, who never knew anything about the RHN
codes, what the 'good groups' were.

If you look systematically at the three-letter code groups
that were actually used in the messages, you will soon
spot the sort of thing to look for. Take the code groups
starting with the letter 'F'. Write them out in alphabetical sequence.

FAP FBH FBY FCS FDI FEM FGH FGV FJR FKZ
FLR FMO FMV FNA FNU FOM FPS FRC FSL FSY
FTN FUZ FVK FWL FXE FXS FYB FZR

This makes a total of twenty-eight groups out of a possible 625! A severe limitation indeed! As explained earlier,
the letter 'Q' was never used in the first position to avoid
confusion with the international Q-code used by amateurs and service operators alike. But 'Q' does not appear
in second or third position either. What other letters are
omitted? Obviously 'F' itself is not repeated either as the
second or the third letter; and it is apparent that no letter
is repeated within a group. Neither FAA nor FBB, nor
yet FFF, nor any such set occurs. Are all the possible sec-

ond letters used? No, 'H' and 'I' are also left out. And in the third position you will find that apart from 'F' itself and 'Q', there is no 'G', 'J', 'T', 'W' or 'X'.

How about the 'G' section?

GAU GBJ GCV GDH GEP GFY GHT GIM GJF GKM GLF GLY GMJ GMK GOI GPF GRV GST GSU GTD GUO GVF GVT GWD GWX GXC GXV GYN GZM

This comprises twenty-nine groups, so is similar in size. Again, no 'Q's or letters are used twice within a group. There are no omitted letters in second position, and in the third no 'A', 'B', 'L', 'R', 'S' or 'W'.

And the 'H's?

HAK HBI HBS KCK HDU HEN HFD HFV HGD HIM HIU HJC HKD HLK HMG HNJ HOZ HPO HRF HRX HSN HTR HVD HWM HXG HXS HYR HZB HZV

This has twenty-nine groups again, with no 'Q's or re-peated letters. Otherwise, only 'U' is omitted in second position within these code phrases, but in third position 'A', 'E', 'H', 'L', 'P', 'T' and 'Y' are absent.

Some code phrases are much less likely than others to be employed, such as 'emergency landing in neutral ter-ritory', while a few would appear in most messages, like 'my location is square such-and-such', and others always at the beginning or end of a sortie. These stereo-typed phrases could easily be identified and the actual three-letter groups memorised, so you did not need to remem-ber the whole set of 'good groups'. A few of the most often encountered ones sufficed to identify an intercepted message as coming from a Luftwaffe bomber aircraft. This 'give-away' feature remained with the RHN code series of encipher sheets, although periodically changing encipherment made recovery of each period's setting less easy. The identification quality vanished once the Luftwaffe went over to the use of a daily changing numerical encipher and decipher sheet. Any three-digit number could occur in any position in any message, seen from the viewpoint of our staff coming on watch and faced with a batch of new traffic.

David, coming in on the morning shift, was required to write on wide sheets for the edification of the rest of his section the meaning of decoded ('recovered' in BP-speak) groups. The tedium of writing out the long phrases from the German soon taught him to abbreviate. '*Mein Standort ist Quadrat #*' (my position is square #) soon became 'S/O #'. If all messages had been perfectly sent and perfectly intercepted, the decoder's task would have been much easier than it actually was. But because of bad weather, poor sending, radio interference or other reasons, whole groups could be lost or distorted, producing garbles – places where the decode did not make sense because a letter had been mistakenly recorded. It was the decoder's task to work out, if possible, the correct message.

At the end of each day all Rhino posses were signalled to the Middle East, where a party had been set up to handle SIGINT (Signals Intelligence) material, and pass it to the few authorised recipients there, and also to process traffic intercepted locally. Such traffic from the Mediterranean was signalled to David's section by secure channels. Meanwhile work on the previous day's take continued, for the messages sent in the Med were different from those in the Channel or the Atlantic, and recoveries made from one source could often be used on another. The traffic dealt with included German meteorological flights, known at BP as 'Zenits'.

It was extremely important for the Luftwaffe (and all branches of the Wehrmacht) to know what the weather was like over the Atlantic and Arctic oceans, because the weather moves from west to east, so early every morning meteorological flights set off from Norway, western France and Italy. At intervals of about fifteen minutes, observations were then relayed back to base, using AuKa code to give the aircraft's location in terms of a grid, followed by weather details in an enciphered variant of the international Met. code. The aircraft's early position reports, soon after departure, usually conformed to an established route, so that the grid squares could be easily filled in, and recovery of the day's RHN setting begin.

It was very necessary to dissuade Coastal Command and Fighter Command from intercepting and shooting down these Zenit flights, but, as usual, without letting them know of the existence of Bletchley Park! Even the German Met. code data were earnestly studied by Lieutenant Doniach (brother of the well-known musician Shula Doniach), because these reports, when converted into plain text, were often relayed by the Germans on different networks using higher-grade ciphers, and they often provided useful cribs. Any message already decoded by BP and later passed on using a different code was of course a gift to the code-breakers.

Other networks dealt with by the sub-section were known as the Western Kreis and the Mediterranean Kreis (German for 'circuit'), on which urgent sightings of convoys appeared. Their position on the grid was followed by numbers of various types of ship, their course and speed. This information was of immediate operational importance, for the enemy would almost certainly seek to attack the convoy by sea and from the air. A warning had to be flashed to the Admiralty and Coastal Command, or, in the Mediterranean, to local commands direct from the BP liaison party in Alexandria.

One of David's fellow workers was a Londoner, stout, pallid and always wearing a conventional black suit, in marked contrast to the sports jackets and flannels worn by most male civilians. He felt himself to be an outsider among the highly educated young ladies and university men, as he had left school at fourteen, so he repelled all friendly overtures and remained in sullen seclusion. This was a pity, as he was a clever man who had educated himself by taking courses in Turkish, German and Japanese. His job was to decode traffic from Staaken aerodrome in East Berlin, from which every day a busy service of Junkers-52 three-engined aircraft (the German counterparts of the famous Dakota) plied eastward to Rastenburg, where Hitler had his 'Wolf's Lair' headquarters for the Russian campaign. The Junkers also flew to various centres in Poland and occupied parts of Russia.

Messages were often sent announcing that VIPs were travelling and where they were bound. From the code-recovery point of view, the names of regular passengers were very useful. A passage which had to spell out names was specially welcome, since you could recover by this means most, if not all, of the alphabet. The names of General Martini (head of the Luftwaffe signals branch) or General Freytag von Loringhoven (Hitler's air force adjutant) were received with acclamation. These gentlemen would have been horrified to know how greatly BP welcomed any reference to them by name. Of course, too, knowledge of their movements, and of those of other important Nazis, could often provide useful hints to the pundits.

The Staaken expert would often refer to a thick ledger containing transport aircraft call signs, which were frequently related to their registration numbers. He had a habit of licking his finger each time he turned a page, until the dog-eared pages turned black and began to smell. At last the Staaken airport was taken over, and the book could be ceremoniously burned in a tin waste-paper basket. The staff in that office were accustomed to handling unpleasant books, because all code books, cipher sheets and other material possibly related to their work were sent to them for examination and retention, having been acquired in various ways, often from aircraft which had been shot down. They might be badly charred, soaked or stained with blood or spattered with fragments of unlucky aircrew. Gradually, however, so many AuKa code books became available that only those in good condition were kept, and the Dirty Books, as they were known, could thankfully be destroyed.

After a few months David was detached from the main section and attached to George T, who was examining material from Luftwaffe units on the Eastern Front, which mainly audible in the Middle East. This reached BP by bag after the lapse of a few days. Probably this was to see whether it would be possible to supply the Air Ministry with statistical summaries of German air activity over Russia, similar to the summaries made for western units so as to complete their picture of actual German operational abilities.

George T was a delightful man, but unfortunately very deaf. As well as David, he had been allotted an RAF typist and a civilian assistant named Marjorie, whom, to stress the Russian note of his small domain, he always called Marjoriewskaya. She and David were found a corner in a small room where they deciphered each day's traffic, using the keys already recovered. As this traffic was absolutely new to BP, they were able to make additional recoveries of cipher key, which had to be transmitted immediately to the main section.

The bomber units on the Russian front behaved on the whole like bomber units in the west, but each had its own idiosyncrasies. Sometimes unusual place names were spelt out, such as the river Psysch, one of whose bridges was a target. The reconnaissance units, however, were much more interesting to the code-breakers. At first there were units based in the Crimea, which flew sorties down the Black Sea coast as far as the Turkish frontier. There were no real convoys there, but they reported in AuKa such shipping as they encountered, as well as Russian naval activity in shipyards such as Batumi.

The type of aircraft employed was the Ju-88, a special high-altitude version of the Ju-88 bomber. Photography was evidently the main purpose of these flights, but reports were sent immediately in case the plane was shot down or the films were of poor quality.

Land reconnaissance, giving close support over battlefields, was done by fighters or by light aircraft such as the Fieseler Storch, similar to the British Lysander. While the Luftwaffe still had some superiority in the air over Russia, it was able to operate long-range reconnaissance with bomber-type aircraft, so David became familiar with a kind of sighting no longer in evidence elsewhere.

One of the squadrons, which specialised in railway reconnaissance, regularly flew along railway lines behind the Russian front, reporting the number of trains seen in each direction, or the estimated number of locomotives and wagons in a railway yard. Locations were specified on a grid, so David put up on the wall in front of his desk a large gridded map, and pencilled in all places where sightings were reported. It was from this map that BP first became aware that the Soviets had built a railway down the east bank of the Volga, beyond the reach of the Germans, to supply Stalingrad while it was under attack. Clusters of rail sightings began to appear down this stretch, where no railway lines were marked on any British map. The Germans were powerless to halt this work, and it probably played a part in the crushing defeat of General Friedrich von Paulus and his army in the winter of 1942–3. Messages often mentioned *'bespannte Fahrzeuge'* (vehicles

with draught animals), for both sides in this area used great
numbers of carts drawn by horses, oxen or even camels.

The units whose messages most often reached David were
numbered 3/F121, 4/F122 and 3/FObd.1. The first number
denoted the squadron, the F stood for *Fernaufklaerungsgruppe*
(long-range reconnaissance wing) and 121 and 122 were the
wing numbers. Obd.1 meant *Oberbefehlshaber der Luftwaffe*,
and that unit was presumably directly under the control of
Reichsmarschall Hermann Goering himself. David suspected
from the various messages transmitted that all these squadrons were sent off indiscriminately on any task that seemed
urgent at the time. There was a special squadron, commanded
by a certain Colonel Theodor Rowehl, which carried out secret missions in peacetime, or, before a planned invasion of
Yugoslavia or Greece, photographed possible targets (rather
like the U-2 flights during the Cold War). BP knew of this
squadron, but, to David's disappointment, never came across
any communications from it. This was understandable, because for secret missions absolute radio silence must be, and
doubtless was, strictly enforced.

Later in 1943, when the Germans were forced to evacuate
the Crimea, an interesting, though not very important, line
of traffic came in. It concerned arrangements for escorts of
barges, towed by tugs, taking supplies from Yevpatoria to the
Rumanian coastal ports on the mouth of the Danube. AR196
seaplanes or Rumanian 1AR aircraft were employed. Messages scheduled the departures for the following day, and often
spelled out the route – Tendra Peninsula, Sagani Lake, Isle of

Serpents and so on. The vulnerable barge convoys kept close to the coast for fear of Soviet ships and submarines, hoping to enjoy the protection – such as could be spared from more vital tasks – of Axis aircraft.

As well as traffic of identified Luftwaffe units, intercept officers sometimes, while searching the wavelengths, came across items which seemed to be, for various reasons, German Air Force-related, and these were submitted to David's section. If they turned out to be new or interesting, Cheadle would be asked to obtain more, if this was possible within the framework of priorities laid down from above. After the war, some books mentioned friction and jealousy between BP, Cheadle, the Y Service and other sites concerned with wartime radio monitoring. David never saw the slightest signs of this, but experienced only good and close co-operation between all these bodies. Initial work done at Cheadle and other sites, both at home and overseas, was followed up, and the results consolidated and circulated by BP, which acted as the co-ordinating authority on this matter.

The pundits who dealt with Enigma often had mathematical ability of a high order, and required in most of the people who worked with them that they should be able to recognise plain text when it emerged, and to know enough of the language to predict, at least partly, what the message content was likely to be. (However, a very distinguished professional cryptographer, when asked what the minimum requirements for a cryptographer should be, replied, 'Oh, I suppose a sharp pencil and some squared paper.') For low-grade analysis, much lower attainments were sufficient. These were a combination of moderate language skills, background knowledge and intuition, built up by experience of particular traffic. In both high- and low-grade work there were many boring and mechanical jobs – copying, indexing, collating and checking – and all had to be done thoroughly and conscientiously by hand, for there were no computers. David was fortunate enough to find his work enthralling, and to do many jobs which were not always simply routine. He enjoyed it enough to be unable to leave it at the end of a shift, and would toil through another eight hours to complete it. He was also acquiring a detailed body of knowledge of certain theatres of war which might be envied by many a field commander.

For me, it is also enthralling to learn from his work how, while great battles were fought and important plans made by High Commands, in the background continued all the dull business of transport, supplies, reconnaissance, photography and the simple ferrying of passengers here and there, without which the historic battles could never have been fought, nor the vital decisions taken.

Chapter 8

Within the Gates

As I stood disconsolate before the great gates of Bletchley Park with my kitbag and haversack on the ground beside me, I felt hungry, tired and utterly unable to think what to do next. This was certainly the strangest posting I had ever encountered. At Chicksands they had been prompt to get rid of me, and here apparently no one wanted me.

The elderly guard had called for help, and it came hurrying towards me out of the gates in the shape of a very tall squadron leader with a limp. The next summer I was to see him at a pathetic little fair that had come to Bletchley; he was sitting on the Giant's Stride with his legs stretched out before him, his swinging seat almost horizontal as it whizzed through the air, his face enraptured. He was evidently reliving his flying days, from which his wound had cut him off.

Now he limped up to me and said rapidly that I was to wait for a ride to Shenley Church End, where I would stay in a hostel for a few days. 'Can't come in till got a pass, see?' he explained, 'got to be vetted, then get pass, eh?' And evidently feeling that he had made all clear, he limped away, back into the haven where I would be. I was only too glad to know that somebody cared about me. In a few minutes another motor-cycle rider roared up, bundled me and my belongings into his sidecar, and took me to the Old Vicarage in the first of the two tiny villages, Shenley Church End and Shenley Brook End, which were a few miles out of Bletchley itself.

Here I and two other girls, neither destined for BP, spent three rather idyllic days, exploring the old house, wandering through its large neglected grounds, eating gooseberries and currants and wishing that we could explore Shenley Brook End, a short distance away. However we had been told not to leave the house or grounds, since no one knew when we would be 'collected'.

A WAAF officer was in nominal charge of us, but she only smiled agreeably when she passed us in the corridor; otherwise she lived in scenes of inconceivable chaos in a large front room. Tables were smothered in open books, bursting files, heaps of paper, plates of mildewed toast, cups with piles of notebooks precariously balanced on top and large photographs scattered indiscriminately overall.

One of my companions at the Old Vicarage told me that, bored with having nothing to do, she had offered to tidy these tables, only to be met with cries of horror. 'Thank you, thank you, my dear,' said the officer, with hardly concealed dismay, 'but I have everything arranged exactly as I like it, and if any-thing were moved I should never be able to find what I need.'

After the war I found out that this lady was a very distinguished Greek epigraphist, who had published several books of seminal importance.

Whatever 'vetting' was, I evidently passed it successfully and was collected by a tall, elegant, rather forbidding, silent woman in FANY (First Aid Nursing Yeomanry) uniform on the morning of the third day, and taken to my billet in Stony Stratford. There, after the briefest of introductions to my landlady, I was told to leave my kit and was hurried on to BP. Again I walked confidently up to the guardhouse, and again I was turned away – by two different guards this time. I was told to go (yet again) to the small hut outside the gates. Soon there appeared a small plump wing commander with a deep bass voice, which became even deeper when he needed to stress something important.

I have a very good memory for words. I had an English teacher who insisted on my learning a fresh poem every week, and soon I found that I could repeat hundreds of poems and hymns, as well as long speeches from Shakespeare (very useful during sleepless nights or long journeys). I have almost no visual memory at all: ask me the day after what someone was wearing, or how a room was furnished, and I am at a complete loss. Yet words, quotations and whole conversations I can remember very well indeed. So in this book I can repeat pretty well what was said on many occasions, and this is what that wing commander said to me in the little hut.

'What I am going to say, corporal,' the wing commander boomed, 'is extremely important.' He looked at me sternly.

'You will be working in the most secret place in Britain, and all the activities here are crucial to the outcome of the war. The work here is so secret that you will be told only what it is necessary for you to know, and you will never, never seek to find out more than you have been told. But besides keeping internal security, you will also be mindful of external security. You will never mention the name of this place, not to your family, not to your friends, not to anyone you may meet. You will find that your colleagues refer to it as BP, and you will find it convenient to do the same. More than this, you will never disclose to anyone the nature of the work that you will be doing; to reveal the least hint could jeopardise the whole progress of the war. Nor will you mention anything about the location of this place, its propinquity to a railway, its nearest town – you will not let any least detail escape you.'

I was rather in awe of this little man, and his speech was so fluent that I thought he must have given it many times, but I felt that I had to interrupt him. 'But, sir,' I said, 'my mother writes to me every week – what shall I tell her?' 'All correspondence will be addressed to your billet,' he replied. 'In case of emergency, a telegram could be sent to Box 101, Bletchley. You can tell your family that you are doing ordinary clerical work, and you will never discuss with anyone outside your own section the work you will be doing, and not with anyone in your section unless your section head gives you permission.' 'And what work will that be, sir?' I said innocently.

It was evidently the wrong thing to say. The little man swelled as though he might explode. 'Good God, girl,' he said, 'haven't you listened to a single word I've said? I know nothing about your work, and I don't expect to know anything. But listen to me now, because what I'm going to say is of the utmost importance.' He took out of the table drawer a piece of rather yellowish paper. 'This is the Official Secrets Act. It clearly states that if, by doing any of the things I have warned you against, you disclose the slightest information which could be of use to the enemy you will be committing TREASON.'

This was pretty strong stuff for an eighteen year old, and I was nervously impressed. I was not reassured when he said quite thoughtfully, 'If you did, you would be liable to the extremest penalties of the law, and I'm not sure whether, at the moment, that's hanging or shooting by firing squad.'

I looked at him anxiously to see whether he was joking, but he put a fountain pen in my hand and motioned me to sign the paper. I read it through, but I had not then, and I have not now, the faintest idea of its contents. I really thought I was in some sort of test, intended to see how I would react. The officer then took back his paper, folded it away and fumbled in a small envelope. 'Here', he said, 'is your pass, which will never, ever, leave your person.' (I had a mental picture of myself in the bath, with the pass between my teeth.) 'You will never show it to anyone, except one of the guards. If it were to be lost or mislaid, the consequences could be disastrous.' He handed me a rectangle of talc-covered stiff board (for plastics were still in the future) and I wondered what to do. Eventually I decided to put it in the breast pocket of my uniform. I found out later that, human nature being what it is, passes were occasionally

mislaid or left at home after leave, and, although the miscre-
ants were no doubt severely reprimanded, the war effort did
not seem in any way to be affected. There was in fact a certain
gentleman in a certain hut who would make you, if you were
desperate, a pass good enough to deceive the guards.

'That, I believe, covers all I have to say to you,' said the wing
commander, rising from his chair. 'We shall probably not meet
again, so I wish you luck, corporal. When you are older, you
will realise what a very great privilege it is to have been selected
to work here. Now come with me.' With my heart beating very
hard, I followed him through the gates – or would have done,
if the guard had not interposed a large hand and intoned 'pass,
please'. I thought they were both laughing at me, but I didn't
care. The wing commander turned back. 'By the way,' he said
to me quietly, 'although you'll be on special duties, we can't
say so, you know. Accounts would want to know why we'd
got so many. So we'll just upgrade you to sergeant. That way
you'll get a bit more pay. And incidentally, if you don't like it
here, don't bother to apply for a posting, because you won't get
one.' He laughed very loudly, a deep bass laugh. 'You won't
get one, because you're here for the duration.'

The Park was a very strange place, once you were inside,
especially for someone who had formerly been posted only to
stations where the extremely rigid and disciplined routine of
an RAF camp went on: parades; uniforms; saluting; saying
'Sir' or 'Ma'am' to officers; and being careful to 'book out' if
you left the camp and book in again when you came in. Then
there were kit inspections, unmaking your bed every morning

and making it up again every night, polishing your floor space, and dozens of other ploys, probably necessary when you had hundreds of people to control, but still exasperating and time wasting. The worst thing of all, for the WAAFs at least, was the monthly FFI (Free From Infection) medical inspections. These were to make sure that every service woman had no lice in her hair, no decay in her teeth and (this was the worst horror) no crabs, no syphilis and no other sexually transmitted disease. Standing in a queue in your knickers while a bored orderly and doctor moved along the line was good healthcare, but terribly humiliating.

In the Park these things simply did not exist. I was amazed at first to find that there were hundreds (thousands actually, but divided into shifts) of civilians, some army officers, a good many naval officers and a lot of WRNS, but apparently only one WAAF – myself! I soon found out that all Air Force personnel were allowed to wear civilian clothes if they wished, and as most did so there was no saluting. We were all in billets, and how we kept our bedrooms and belongings was presumably between our landladies and ourselves. More RAF personnel did wear uniform in winter, because it was warmer than our pre-war civilian clothes (though for many of us our school uniforms comprised most of our clothes other than Air Force uniform). Even if you did wear uniform, there was no saluting because you worked in rooms with officers who became your friends, or at least acquaintances, and it would have seemed ridiculous to salute them. As to leaving the Park, you could do so whenever you were free, just as long as you showed your pass when it was time to go back in. What you did in the village or town where you were billeted, no one knew or cared. You had to inform your section head where you would be on your long leave – one whole week! – but for your days off you were as free as a bird. I don't know what you did if you wanted to see a doctor, because I never needed to, but I am sure you didn't have to go on Sick Parade. Possibly there was a ceremony of lowering the flag at sunset and playing 'Lights Out', but I don't know where.

The exception to all this free living were the navy personnel. The Admiralty required them at all times to be smartly dressed, to conform to all navy regulations, to attend parades and even to do drill! I heard that some WRNS who were working on the bombes, which after the war we found out was the most excruciating physical labour in the Park, actually lived in an old country mansion where there were mice in the gravy and swallows flew in and out of the broken windowpanes. They still had to salute the quarterdeck (usually the area in front of the huge country houses they lived in).

Some of the army, too, wore uniform, but mostly they worked in a distant part of the grounds, and we saw little of them. Their camp was being built at some time after I arrived, and we greatly pitied the ATS girls who would have to go back to camp routine. Little did we know (as romantic novels say) that in another year we WAAF too would be subjected once again to all the horrors of a proper RAF station!

Chapter 9

Making Friends

AT FIRST, I THOUGHT I WAS quite unlucky to be taken to the hut where Mr B ruled so benignly. There were several delightful people in the hut (whose number neither David nor I can remember), but what really bad luck to have a section head who was an enigma in himself, whose codes no one ever managed to crack! He was not an unpleasant man – quite the contrary. He was a kind and caring boss, who almost never lost his temper, and always tried to keep the young girls on the day shift, since he did not like to think of them walking home through the blacked-out streets. If you were a little late back from lunch he might raise an eyebrow, but you would have to be very late before he remonstrated. He was a small thin man with the face of an intelligent monkey, and had a pipe which he sucked lovingly but seldom lit.

Why, then, was this kind little man such a disaster to newcomers to his section? A head was supposed to explain what to do, to inform, to elucidate, to advise. Mr B could not do any of these things, because he had two fatal flaws. The first, and lesser, was that he had a sudden spasmodic smile which flashed across his face at very short intervals, regardless of the subject of his conversation at the time. The British – or at least the English – are conditioned to smile when smiled at, and it took time for newcomers to realise that this was a mere rictus or twitch, requiring no answering smile. It was disconcerting in the extreme to feel an idiot smile on one's face, while Mr B's had become instantaneously as solemn as a judge's, or to be rudely blank as he flashed his radiant grin. But this was a mere idiosyncrasy. After a few weeks, one simply did not notice the smile appearing and disappearing like the beam from a light-house. It was just one of BP's many variations from the norm which were first accepted and then forgotten; they ceased to exist in one's consciousness. This was a good thing, because high intelligence, often near genius, did seem to be accompanied by an enormous number of eccentricities, twitches, peculiarities and obsessions; these were accepted tolerantly and often, in time, affectionately.

In any case, this small grimace of Mr B's paled before his other disability, for he could not make himself understood. It was not that he had a speech defect; no, he spoke in the Oxbridge accent common at BP, and pronounced his words clearly and well. It was just that after the first sentence or two the listener realised he or she had not the faintest idea of what Mr B was talking about. It was like reading the second page of J. W. Dunne's *An Experiment in Time*. You set off confidently and realised almost at once that you were completely at sea.

The sentences rolled mellifluously off the tongue, but made no sense. They made sense to the speaker, because he accompanied them with emphatic explanatory gestures, but to the listener all was mystery.

When I first realised that I had no idea what my new boss was talking about, I thought it must be my fault. Perhaps the extreme confusion resultant on the posting to Bletchley had actually affected my mind. I was evidently being given an introductory talk, and he was probably explaining what my work would be. It was terribly important that I grasp his meaning through the fog of unfamiliar words that surfaced from the rapid flow, which included words such as 'intercepts', 'cryptanalysis' and '*Schuesselblaetter*'. When the flow ceased, he gave me a real, encouraging smile. 'You see?' he said, and I could only answer feebly 'I think so.' It was a lie. What I wanted to say was 'I really didn't understand a word. Could you say that all over again, and very, very slowly, stopping at the end of every sentence so that I can ask you if I don't understand?' But, of course, this was not the sort of thing one said to a new boss. In a normal work situation I would simply have been told that I wasn't suitable for the job, but I had been told that I was here 'for the duration'. It was a nightmare situation. Mr B led me to a seat at one of the tables, on which there was a small pile of papers, put a pencil into my hand and, with a last bright smile, went back to his chair and table, which was positioned like a teacher's desk at the front of the room.

The classroom structure reminded me horribly of a scene in my kindergarten. It was the last time I had felt as helpless as this. My class had each been given a pair of child-sized wooden knitting needles with some stitches already cast on. The teacher then, with a pair of giant needles, showed the children how to wind the wool round the needle, make a stitch and transfer it to the other needle. She repeated this action slowly and carefully until she came to the end of the row, then showed how to change needles and repeat the making of stitches. She asked if everyone understood. I, who at six was halfway through Rudyard Kipling's *Kim*, was too cowardly to say that I didn't understand at all. When all the other tots began busily to knit, I spent the lesson slowly moving the existing stitches from one needle to another, having never grasped the movements involved. Everyone else's bit of knitting grew longer; only mine remained the same size. The details of the eventual exposure had been mercifully expunged from my mind, but, here, now, in this place so crucial to the war effort, the same ignominious situation was repeated. Everyone else would clear his pile of paper, while I would sit shuffling mine about. And what, what would take the place of the teacher's exasperation at the discovery of my cowardice and ineptitude – some politer but inconceivably more humiliating scene? I thought I had never been more miserable in my life. Mr B, in his haste to introduce me to the delights of decoding, had not thought to introduce me to anyone else, but this was BP where no introductions were needed.

The young man sitting opposite me at the table leaned over and asked if I needed any help, and with a surge of gratitude I said 'yes, I needed to know everything, but first of all what was

I to do?' He said that his name was Denys, and he showed me the code book by the pile of paper and how it worked. All the traffic had already been reciphered – turned from its three-letter groups into the original three-figure groups, which had to be looked up in the code book (with rather sinister brown stains on its edges) and the decode written in pencil beneath. Where there were blanks or garbles, you could either guess at what was meant or leave a blank. I had been given a pile of what were called tuning messages. These were sent out at the beginning of operations, to make sure that they were in contact with the station they wanted to communicate with.

The base controller often sent what looked like a genuine message which, when decoded, spelled out 'this is a tuning message.' Sometimes, hoping to inspire the troops, he would send some well-known German proverb, and Denys showed me how easy it might be to guess what a blank or garbled group was saying. For instance, if you got a slip saying '*Morgen*(blank) (blank) *Gold im M*(blank blank blank)*e*' and you knew the saying, or even if you didn't, you knew what was missing. The complete slip was simply saying '*Morgenstunde hat Gold im Munde*' (early morning has gold in its mouth) – a rough equivalent of our 'early to bed, early to rise'. Denys also told me that, when I was used to traffic from one particular station, I would learn to recognise what it was saying because it had become familiar. This was very comforting, and turned out be true.

Mr B kept us all doing traffic from the same stations every day, and although this could become boring, especially if your traffic was saying pretty much the same kind of thing all the time, you did develop a sort of intuition about its messages. Also, when a colleague went on leave, another member of the section had to take over his traffic, which created some variety.

I soon got to know the other members of our small section. Mr B, as head, worked only the day shift. His job was to examine all the slips which had been decoded as far as possible and decide what should be done with them. Anything he thought to be of real interest or importance went higher up; any mention of new ships, aircraft, places, persons or new technology went for indexing. Traffic which had hardly been decoded at all was left for a later shift, when more kracks would have come in, though Mr B was remarkably skilful himself at making further decodes, which he seemed to do by intuition rather than reason. But it was no use asking how he did it, because he would tell you, and after you had listened uncomprehending you were no wiser than before. By a very happy arrangement his best friend was George T, and one often saw them walking or eating together, the one talking rapidly and earnestly, the other hearing little and probably understanding less, but smiling benignly, both pleased with each other's company.

By far the most extraordinary person in the section was Maurice Zarb, a tall, skeletal man with rather a skull-like face, but certainly the most cultured and knowledgeable person I had ever met. His father was Maltese with some Greek ancestry, and his mother the daughter of an Arab princess who had married an Egyptian, so that Maurice spoke more languages than he could remember. He read omnivorously in many of them, and always maintained that the Russians were the greatest novelists, though he admitted that English poetry was among the greatest in the world. He would sometimes quote eastern love poetry, which he said was the most sensuous, just as he believed that Mozart's music was the most amorous. Conversation with Maurice was like being fed with delicious and fascinating food – you always wanted more of it. It showed too a kind of sophistication, a knowledge of the world which was illuminating to me, an eighteen year old who had never been abroad and had read mostly books approved by a school. After talking to him, I always felt that my mind had actually physically expanded. He was endlessly kind, too, with newcomers; but now that I am older I think that he found the British rather limited in some ways, even the brilliant people at Bletchley. His experience of life had been so extensive, and theirs often confined to public school and university. He was very far, however, from being a snob, in spite of his half-royal birth, and his prestigious position in the Crédit Lyonnais, in the world of international banking, of which even his friends knew nothing until after the war. In fact, it was the RAF which was snobbish. Because presumably of his mixed ancestry, he was never even recommended for a commission, which he must have found sardonically amusing.

Denys, my first helper, could hardly have had a more different upbringing and background from Maurice. His father had been killed either just before or just after Denys was born, and he had become, while still almost a baby, his young mother's aid and support – the man of the house. However, he had two great alleviations in this arduous life: he followed the fortunes of Arsenal with enormous interest, and he passionately loved and knew every note of many Italian operas. His favourite composer was Bellini, then very little known, and I can still hum arias from some of his operas, which instantly bring back Denys's absorbed and blissful face. He had carried, when still a boy, more burdens than the majority of those at Bletchley, where a privileged lifestyle had been the norm. He had an enormous collection of records, the old tremendously heavy seventy-eights, and to these he hurried back on his day off with anticipations of heavenly happiness. Although still in his early twenties, Denys was a serious young man, but would sometimes be surprised by a joke into a spasm of uncontrollable laughter.

Another member of Mr B's team was a dark, silent man with a heavy moustache, to whom Maurice would often chat in a – to me – unknown language. With all the brazen curiosity of youth, I asked Maurice about this. He told me that our colleague was Paul Fetterlein, and that his father (also at BP, though in a more exalted section) had been chief code-breaker to the tsar of Russia and had escaped during the revolution to join British Intelligence. This story held all the romance of a novel to me, and I would look with awe at its hero.

The only other female member of our room was a lady, perhaps in her thirties, who wore what were then very strange clothes – a kind of long kaftan, with a scarf twisted round her head to make a turban. She usually held herself rather aloof, but would sometimes, when most of the others were at lunch, pour out to me a long lament about her lost happiness, and her yearning to get back to the Cambridge ladies' college where she had been a professor of eastern languages. In winter she would pile scarves and shawls on top of her kaftan, and huddle against the lukewarm radiator rubbing her gloved hands. At some time in 1943 she disappeared, whether to some other department, or to leave because of illness, I never knew. I never saw her about the Park, but she always remained a glamorous figure to me, who had never been even to Ireland or France, and had never imagined living in eastern lands.

One morning Mr B made a short announcement to the section, with smiles flashing round the room, at which Maurice looked amused, and began one of his long silent laughs. I asked what Mr B had said, and Maurice replied that 'our poet' was returning after having been on a commission course, which he had failed. I was agog to hear of this new arrival, since poetry was a great passion of mine and I had never met a real poet. The next morning, rather after the rest of us had arrived, the door opened and a smiling face looked round. A general gasp went up, for the head was completely shaven, a thing I had never seen in my life. Convicts had their head shaved to prevent lice, but were always allowed to grow hair again for a month before their release. The poet came in, walking in a springy way as though on heather. He was slight and lithe, and seemed to be amused at being back. All work stopped. Even Mr B looked up and took his pipe out of his mouth. The following conversation took place. (I remember it well, it was my first introduction to a poet.)

'Why do you look like a criminal?' said Maurice accusingly, 'and why are you not an officer?'

'Ah,' said this strange man thoughtfully, 'ah, well, that may have been a bit my fault. I thought I was doing quite well. I got top marks in rifle and revolver shooting, and you know I've got a good memory, so I did well in the written exams too. It was the drill that let me down. I marched my squad into a brick wall. I just forgot to say "about turn", and the fools deliberately went on marching.' There was a general scream of laughter. 'And I may have made a bit of a hash in my final interview. The air commodore asked me why I went on the passing-out parade without my rifle. I told him there were so many things to think of, I really couldn't remember everything, and I told him he'd no idea how difficult it was to present arms without a rifle. He seemed a bit impressed by this, I thought. But then he said I'd had a book of poems published, hadn't I? He seemed rather supercilious about it, so I said did he think that an unsuitable thing to do in war-time? He said he hoped I wasn't writing any more while I was serving in the RAF. I replied that as a matter of fact I wrote poems all the time, because what poets wrote about war was far more important than what historians wrote. I may have quoted a bit of Wilfred Owen, and some David Jones – out of *In Parenthesis*, you know. Then the wing commander said he thought they'd heard enough now to make a decision, and he dismissed me. He seemed a bit upset, I thought,' said this strange man in a wondering tone. 'But', he said, 'I didn't really want to be an officer anyway. You get much better table tennis in the sergeants' mess.' He turned to Mr B. 'I expect', he said, 'after I've been away so long that someone else has taken over my traffic, so what have you got for me to do now?' But Mr B, with flashing smiles, replied that he wouldn't think of giving it to anyone else, and handed over a large bundle of slips, which was received with a groan. I hurried to my seat, and hastily scribbled as much of this conversation as I could remember, to be copied into my notebook that evening. It would go well, I thought, in the great comic novel I was going to write after the war about life in the Air Force.

It was not until many years after the war that I found out about the traffic our poet hated so much. It was called 'Wim', because it was used by a small special-purpose long-wave unit commanded by a Lieutenant Wimmer. The unit dealt with intercept, tracking and jamming of Allied airborne radar in the western Mediterranean. Their HQ was in the area of Naples, Capri and Portofino, so they almost certainly had a much more comfortable time than the poor wretches on the Eastern Front. For this reason, and because their traffic consisted largely of figures for which he had an extraordinary facility, our poet hated it with venom. He continually begged Mr B to put him on to some other traffic, but always without success.

Chapter 10
Living Quarters

THE PARK WAS A SOCIABLE PLACE, and, despite the difficulties of transport, people liked to meet their friends when they were not working. The most popular places to meet were the country pubs, where there was very moderate drinking (until the Americans arrived, and they mostly brought their own) and where you could play darts, shuffleboard, shove ha'penny or whatever game the landlord kept under the bar. I vividly remember a game of Ludo played with Constantine FitzGibbon and his elegant Irish wife Theodora. She made her indignation known over the infamous rule that a player must throw a six before his counter could begin to play. She was listened to with great respect by the locals, who thought such fiery language a prerogative of the aristocracy, and admired it accordingly.

But sometimes people wished for a quieter or more private meeting, and you might be invited to their billet. In this way you learned how varied were the quarters in which our friends and acquaintances lived 'for the duration'. The luckiest ones were those who had arrived earliest in Bletchley, and thus had a choice of places to stay before the crowds moved in.

The eccentric elder code-breaker Dillwyn (always known as Dilly) Knox lived in the cottage in the stable yard at BP, where he worked. 'The walls were coated with whitewash,' wrote his niece Penelope Fitzgerald. '. . . The two downstairs rooms were connected by a cupboard, which Dilly frequently mistook for the door. His voice could be heard inside, resounding hollowly . . . He could have coffee with real milk, supplied to him by a lady who lived nearby and kept her own cow.' Once a week on his day off he drove to his home.

There were many small private hotels or pubs which had accommodation. The most celebrated of these was the Duncombe Arms in Great Brickhill, where so many dons had such an uproarious time that it was called the Drunken Arms. Stuart Milner-Barry, Hugh Alexander and Gordon Welchman, pundits of Hut Six, lived in the Shoulder of Mutton at Old Bletchley, where they were extremely comfortable, though Welchman and his wife later took a beautiful panelled house in Stony Stratford, where they lived in a very civilised way, giving weekly musical evenings at which a string quartet played in the lovely panelled drawing room.

Married men often succeeded in finding places for their wives and families to join them, since there were many small cottages whose owners were in the Forces and were glad to rent to reliable tenants. Mr B rented a cottage in Bow Brickhill where he invited members of his section to tea. It was charming in the summer, when I visited, with a large garden where

Canterbury bells grew among the cabbages and sunflowers in the currant bushes, while the walls were covered with roses and honeysuckle. But I thought it would be difficult to live there in the winter with three small children, one cold-water tap, a coal oven and an outside lavatory. I was amused to see that the eldest child, a serious seven year old, evidently numbered 'Daddy' with her two smaller charges, while she and 'Mummy' ran the show.

Our poet lived in the small terraced house of a railwayman's widow in New Bradwell. He was pursued by her daughter, whom she described as 'a big, fond girl', and who longed to be married. When the young Philip Larkin came from Oxford to visit, she cast yearning eyes on him, and invited him to bring his fellow students to see her, but Philip was nervous and seemed deeply interested in her pet goat, who lived at the bottom of the garden.

Captain Daniel Jones was a doctor of literature, doctor of music, composer, polymath and mentor of Dylan Thomas, who had described him as 'Dan, whose future's stranger than ever, his multiplying, harassed women trailing children like seaweed, his symphonies shouldering out in his head to unplayable proportions, his officer's trousers kept up now by three safety pins.' He worked in the Japanese Section, and in the billeting lottery he had drawn the jackpot. He lived in one end of a large farmhouse in Stewkley, which had perhaps been the stockman's quarters, or a big tackroom. It had been made comfortable by the farmer's wife, who had strewn sheepskins and rugs over the stone-flagged floor, laid a goose-feather

I always thought this was remarkably like Josh. Do you agree?

"Tell me, are you a believer in elemental disproportion or de-energised statics, or do you just stick to the Propkoffer theory?"

This cartoon by 'Pont' is an almost photographic likeness of J. E. S. Cooper (Josh), who founded the German Air Section. No photograph of Josh is shown in any of the books about Enigma, as far as I know. (from The British Character, by Pont; Collins, London, 1938)

The author (as Sergeant G. M. Davies, German Air Section) on arrival at Bletchley Park, May 1942. Her sergeant's stripes have not yet been issued to her

Sergeant Robert Hivnor, US Army Intelligence Corps; German Air Section, Bletchley Park, 1943–5

Photograph taken by Vernon Watkins of his fellow code-breakers in Hut Fifty-four, RAF Church Green (so named to avoid any connection with Bletchley Park)

David Wendt (right) with a friend in Bletchley Park days

This cartoon on the importance of not being intellectual pinpoints why the intellectuals at Bletchley Park got on so well with one another. In the middle and upper classes in pre-war days, high intelligence was regarded as an unfortunate condition, which was best avoided – even though luckily not catching

Certificate of Discharge from the RAF. Was this WARNING issued only to airmen and airwomen engaged in secret work?

Flight Sergeant Vernon Watkins with the author (his wife Gwen) and his daughter, while still not demobilised from an almost empty Bletchley Park, January 1946

Letter from Vernon Watkins to fellow code-breaker Janet Downs, in February 1946, thanking her for taking a watch to a French friend. He had left it behind when rushing to France to join the army, and then the Resistance. The drawing, by Janet, is of Vernon at Bletchley Park

HOWEVER, MY REASON FOR WRITING, OR IN THIS PRINTING, IS THAT I TOLD THE EDITOR OF A BOSTON MAGAZINE — NOT THE PARTISAN REVIEW — THAT I WOULD REVIEW A BOOK PUT OUT BY THE OXFORD U PRESS CALLED "CODEBREAKERS" RN by HINSLEY & STRIPP WITHOUT HAVING READ IT. NOW I HAVE IT. IT'S A GOOD BOOK. ENGROSSING, BUT NOT AS IT PROFESSES, "THE INSIDE STORY OF BLETCHLEY PARK."

HAVE YOU READ IT?

IF SO I WOULD BE INTERESTED IN YOUR RESPONSE TO THE 29 TESTIMONIALS — NONE BY POETS — MOST ARE HISTORIANS OR TECHNICIANS — WHICH MAKE UP THE BOOK. IT'S ODD BUT DURING THE TIME I KNEW VERNON HE NEVER DISCUSSED ISP NOT IN LETTERS OR CONVERSATION, OF COURSE WE ALL KNEW OF THE OFFICIAL VOW OF SILENCE. BUT STILL.

THIS BRINGS ME TO THE LETTERS OF VW TO ME. ALL DO OR GO OR THE THEM REPOSE IN TEXAS. AT THE UNIVERSITY OF

HARRY RANSOM HUMANITES RESEARCH CENTER
BOX 7219
AUSTIN, TEXAS 78713

ROLLIE McKENNA PUT ME ON TO BRINNON WHO PUT ME ON TO A MAN WHO TOLD ME THEY COLLECTED MODERN BRIT. POETRY.

ANOTHER BOOK OF LESS INTEREST, "THE SELECTED LETTERS OF DELMORE SCHWARTZ & JAMES LAUGHLIN" ed by ROBT PHILLIPS (1993). VERNON IS MENTIONED, I AM CALLED A BAD EGG OR AN EGG THAT DOES NOT COODLE WELL!

GWEN, THIS IS NOT A CHRISTMAS CARD BUT WE WISH YOU AND ALL YOUR YOUNG A MERRY CHRISTMAS.

Bob Hivnor

Letter from Robert Hivnor to the author about Codebreakers, December 1994

The Garth,
Pennard Cliffs,
Near Swansea.

17th May, 1960.

Gentlemen!

Silence, please! Whether my predecessor is making money from old rope or has a job which is a piece of cake is not disclosed, but I welcome the news of him and his family. When I last saw him he had all the makings of a billiards professional, but his letter and the Dundee postmark suggest more prosperous things.

It was good to have news of you all. I am probably the only one of us who asked the way to his own hut while standing in it, and finished his career by travelling home while all his luggage remained in the station cloakroom at Cardington. Life has continued in this laborious pattern up to the date of this letter. But what, it may be wondered by those who remember my first words, distinguishes me from a Trappist monk? Five children instantly spring to the mind after three of them have sprung all day on our remaining chairs. And my wife reminds me that I am to give a talk at Shrewsbury this week-end. Whether my audience will feel that two distinguishing marks are excessive I don't know, but I have a painter friend here whose counsel for living is: 'Keep your bowels open, and your trap shut!' I am not a painter.

Finding that I have done nothing very constructive for this occasion, I bring this note to an untimely close. Denys will be interested to know that I saw the Swans' defeat by Aston Villa with a school friend and my eldest son, who was much the best behaved of us, - my first football match outside this garden for many years. Last Wednesday I spoke to Maurice Zarb on the 'phone. He is head of the legal department of the Crédit Lyonnais in Lombard Street, while provincial banking (Lloyds) is well represented by me, though my nameplate and the slogan 'Bank with Watkins, the Cashier with a Difference!' have disappeared from the counter.

Roy Knight, who is French Professor at Swansea University and appropriately bearded, is probably the only other Bletchley survivor here you would remember. Unless you remember Neville Masterman, history lecturer here, who was in the Army and was so short-sighted that, when he was paid in a gale on a cliff at Land's End, most of his notes blew away over the Atlantic. He was an aircraft-spotter. Neville and Maurice were the two thinnest men in Bletchley. When Neville played the Ghost in the University production of 'Hamlet' this same painter friend said that he would have to train for the part, and put on a bit of weight.

What, I wonder, became of the original T-Lescope? And is it even now having repercussions? Perhaps Denis Costigan's talk was about bird-watching. I last saw him in the company of two wrens. Will future issues of Hut 54 Journal disclose the answer? I should also like news of Charles Hodge who wrote under such difficulties among us. Ah, there is one more person, very little changed, who camped on our lawn with his wife and two sons last Summer, whom we were very glad to see again. It is only nine months since David went.

I end with very best wishes to you all from Gwen and me. And thanks for the Journal which interested us more than Summit.

Kenmor

A 1960 issue of the Hut Fifty-Four *journal annually sent to, and with contributions by, its former inmates. The journal continued until at least 1967, when Vernon Watkins died*

Letter from Janet Downs to the author, after seeing the Darlow Smithson TV programme Station X, *March 1999*

David Wendt in Victoria. Australia, 2004, looking like Isaiah

mattress and a wonderful patchwork quilt over the four-poster bed, and made sure that a great stock of kindling was piled outside. There was an old-fashioned fireplace with a hob, on which a kettle could simmer all day, and a swinging bar on which you could hang an iron pot. In this Captain Jones, a keen and innovative cook, made stews, soups and curries out of strange materials, such as squirrel and snails boiled in wild garlic. He said that he wanted to make sure that he could support himself off the land if there was an invasion, or if rationing got worse. In fact he had no idea of what rationing was at all, since he ate with the family: thick rashers and fresh eggs for breakfast, and chicken, rabbit or pork for lunch or supper. Besides this, the farmer's daughters pressed countless small tributes on him, such as scones, potato cakes and pots of jam. The poet and I went to an evening meal there once, and we had home-made sausages of inconceivable deliciousness, jacket potatoes with butter and fresh broad beans, with a currant tart to follow. We reeled from the table feeling that we had reverted to pre-war days. Captain Jones followed this repast with a salad of chickweed and dandelion leaves, saying that he knew he would never starve if he had to take to the hills.

David Wendt lived in a small redbrick terraced house in Wolverton, with a minute space in front, hardly big enough to call a garden. The back room was the kitchen–living room with its coal-burning range, where the family spent most of their time, since the front room was the cherished 'parlour' of the poor. However this one was used, because it contained a piano which the landlady frequently played. A door out of the kitchen into a back yard with a shed and a lavatory completed the ground floor. As David pointed out, he was used to an outside toilet, since at Trinity he had had to go downstairs and into the basement of the next staircase for relief. His bedroom was sufficiently furnished with a bed and a chest of drawers.

Wolverton had a church and some shops in one of which on Tuesdays you could get buns with a few currants in, or a shaved doughnut with a smear of jam inside. When I was on the four o'clock shift I used to go in on an early bus to queue for these delights. You could also go to lectures organised by the local Workers' Educational Association, and there was a sports ground with a clubhouse, where David could play darts and chat with the locals, though, as this was the first time he had met socially with people from a different background it was difficult to find common subjects or perspectives.

I was billeted in Stony Stratford, a small village consisting of little more than the High Street, which contained a church, a school and a great many pubs, from the Cock at one end of the street to the Bull at the other. There must have been a shop, but I never discovered it, and there was a small Services club, where you could get baked beans on toast in the evenings, and listen to the piano. There were lanes wandering off on each side of the High Street, bordered by the flat fields of Bucking-hamshire. Some of the younger men had been called up, yet even in wartime a semblance of normality prevailed, because most of the local men were railwaymen or agricultural work-ers, both reserved occupations. They came home after their long shifts, ate a meal and then patiently went out again to

Home Guard duties, firewatching, or to work in their allot-
ments or gardens. This was a hard life, but at least most of the
children saw their fathers for a short time each day. The children went to school and Sunday school, to Brownies, Guides
and Scouts with other children whom they had known all their
lives. The women met at the church hall in their scanty free
time to roll bandages, to make jam or bottle whatever fruits
were in season, with their government allocation of sugar.
How the women fed and clothed their families under wartime
restrictions and shortages was a mystery to me. None of them
had bathrooms. All water had to be heated over a coal fire, and
few of them had gas cookers. All washing was done by hand,
and ironed with old-fashioned flat irons. I had been brought
up in a town, and thought these women led lives of grinding
poverty, yet they seemed always cheerful and good-tempered,
accustomed to helping each other out in childbirth, sickness
or trouble of any sort.

I knew all this because I was billeted with a saint – an old
lady who had lived in the village all her life, from a time when
it had been much smaller and every family knew every other
family. She was a Mrs Gladys Henson, though until the day
we parted with tears I always called her Mrs Henson, and she
called me 'miss'. She had no idea that she was a saint; indeed,
I don't think she thought very much about herself at all. She
thought she was a very lucky woman, although she had left
school at twelve to become a 'weeding woman' and then a
milkmaid, and had been widowed when her only child was
quite young. She told me that it had been a struggle to pay the

rent and feed and clothe her small daughter, 'but the dear Lord helped me wonderful.' I thought at first that this potentate was the local grandee, who perhaps owned her house, but no. He turned out to be the deity Himself. Mrs Henson's life was a constant paean of praise to Him. He it was who had caused the house next door to become vacant, so that her daughter could move in with her family.

The house I was billeted in was one of eight small terraced houses in a short lane with the Vicarage at the High Street end and fields at the other end. The vicar, when he had arrived about ten years before, had not been prepared to put up with the primitive sanitation enjoyed or endured by the previous vicar, but in order to get mains drainage he had to pay for its installation in the whole terrace. At the same time he had electricity installed, so that the primitive little houses had at least some modern conveniences, which Mrs Henson could never be sufficiently grateful for. I suspect that she saw the hand of the dear Lord in these improvements. The house itself consisted of four small rooms, divided by a narrow staircase. The room that Mrs H lived in was a kind of kitchen–living room, with a stone sink under the window and a coal range; it reminded me instantly of Tom Kitten's kitchen. The other front room was the cherished 'parlour', never lived in, never used except for weddings and funerals, and always kept dusted and polished. After I had been her lodger for about three weeks, Mrs H led me in ceremonially and said, 'You can have this, miss, for your writing and that.' I never realised until much later what a sacrifice this was for her, but she had the greatest respect for literacy. She could read, slowly, and greatly enjoyed after her day's work sitting down to look through her son-in-law's newspaper, but writing was a great trial to her, and she needed help with official forms and notices. So she regarded my adolescent scribblings with deep reverence, and I should have liked to tell her that the heroine of my great war novel had changed from being a brave and beautiful girl in the Services to a little old woman who would have made any sacrifice to save a child from suffering.

When she found out that I did not take tea or sugar she was aghast, and made up tiny packets for me to take home to my mother, but I refused, saying she must add them to her own meagre rations. After that, when I came off shift at four o'clock, I often found a shrivelled old lady crouching over the table, or by the fire in winter, gloating over a pot of tea and a few biscuits. I accused my landlady of giving away the tea and sugar, but she explained anxiously, 'You see, miss, if you lives on your own, you only has the one book, and you can't make a good cup after Thursday, no matter how.' It was impossible to make her keep anything for herself. If I gave her a bar of chocolate from the NAAFI (Navy, Army, and Air Force Institute) stores, she said with beaming smiles, 'Oh, miss, the children will enjoy that.' My mother had a neighbour who kept hens, and she was often given some cracked eggs, with which she could make cakes and puddings. Sometimes I would come back from leave bringing a cake specially baked for Mrs H, but immediately she would invite her family and me to tea, watching us with great enjoyment as we ate her cake.

I cannot think of another elderly woman who would have taken a chattering, careless, self-absorbed teenager into her small home and put up with all my thoughtlessness, without a single remonstrance. There was never the least shadow of a difference or disagreement between us, and when I had to leave I did at least realise, young and silly as I was, that I had for once in my life experienced the purest goodness in a human being.

Many years later, when my own children were grown up, I found myself near Bletchley, and decided on an impulse to visit the place where I had been so happy. Dear Mrs H had been dead these many years, and her family dispersed. I did not think Vicarage Walk could have changed a great deal, but it had. It was full of parked cars, and expensive bicycles lay about in the lane. The sacred front doors, never opened except to admit the entrance of a bride or the departure of a coffin, were wide open, and the windows I had never seen open had bright chintz curtains fluttering in the breeze, and from them the sounds of television programmes blared out. Teenagers stood about giggling and listening to transistor radios. Was it better or worse? I didn't know. I only wished that it had not changed. I turned away, and never went there again.

Chapter 11

Changes

IT HAD BECOME OBVIOUS very quickly that the huts did not provide enough working space for the growing numbers of BP
workers, so in 1942 two two-storey buildings were built on the
north side of the lake, called respectively A Block and B Block.
Then followed C and D Blocks, and in the late spring of 1943
F Block was completed, and Mr B led his little band out of the
hut which had housed us so uncomfortably for so long. It had
been both chilly and stuffy in winter and baking in summer,
and we left it without regret.

F Block was furthest from the mansion, the canteen and
the transport collection point, but it was nearest to the private
lane which led from the back of the Park to the railway station. If you slipped out of your section at five minutes to four
(having brought in your weekend bag) and ran as fast as you
could down the lane, you stood a good chance of catching the
train from Birmingham which was supposed to arrive at three
ten but nearly always ran late. Or you could stroll down in a

leisurely fashion and catch the four ten to Euston, which nearly always came in before half-past four.

This was not the only advantage to the move. Instead of the cramped quarters of the hut, we now occupied a spacious sunny room with real radiators that worked and windows that could be opened. There was a work surface round two corners of the room and gleaming new metal tables in the centre, while Mr B sat surveying his domain from a shallow dais at the front. And if you became weary of this luxurious accommodation, you could walk up and down the wide corridors outside, either to rest your eyes and back, or to dabble about in the shining new washroom, where there was real rationed soap, or simply to see what was going on in the BP world.

In this wide light corridor, you might see the two Fetterleins, father and son, now united in the same building, in affectionate conversation. Or you might see 'Cleo' Welsford (so called because her real name, Enid, did not seem to express her haughty temper), a noted Renaissance scholar, steaming along in pursuit of some malefactor who had not returned the *Bird Book*. This was a weighty tome, compiled in the early days with enormous effort by the members of Sixta (an abbreviation of Hut Six Traffic Analysis), which recorded all Luftwaffe three-letter call signs, and in some marvellous way predicted their midnight changes. Perhaps Cleo had been involved in its compilation, for she had a kind of possessive feeling about it. During a lecture she was giving about its use, she had once thrown the Bird Book at the poet, who was preoccupied with a difficult metre at the time. Accustomed in his Gower home to avoiding the attacks of nesting sea birds, he had adroitly leaned away, and it stunned an unlucky flight sergeant dozing in the row behind.

In the corridor you might catch a glimpse of Hugh Alexander, the gifted mathematician and chess champion, on one of his rare visits to the German Air Section. He was much given to Anglo-Saxon attitudes, and when standing to chat would wind one long leg round the other and make strange gestures with his hands. Perhaps he had come to visit one of the never-seen denizens of MI6, who had their lair down one spur, at which we looked fearfully as we passed. Or you might meet Beanie, attractive queen of all stationery stores, hurrying along with piles of papers, stopping only to quote satirically from the latest Mary Webb novel. This lady's books, which became popular only after her death, were full of lust, drama and passion from the county of Shropshire, and Beanie used them only as source books for her own sardonic form of humour. 'The maister be come,' Beanie would say on seeing Mr B returning from lunch. 'It mun be toërts, not frommit,' she would hiss, thrusting a bundle into your unwilling hands. 'His banner over us be love,' she would intone solemnly as Josh stumped past, oblivious of everything but his own weighty thoughts.

Sometimes Josh would be accompanied by a high-ranking official from some Ministry, and would suddenly dart away down a nearby spur. When he returned (it might be after one minute, it might be after ten) he would take up the conversation at the very word with which it had been cut off. Once he appeared, very unusually, in a new suit, and his secretary was heard to say, 'Gosh, Josh, how posh!' Yes, the corridor was the Grand Trunk Road of German Air. All human life was there.

But the new room was fascinating too. Mr B's eyes gleamed as he surveyed his enlarged empire, and the lighthouse beam of his smiles flashed over his new recruits. One of the very few Bletchley drones now made his appearance in our section, probably transferred by some other section head who had despaired of getting any work out of him. Charles H was a short, bulky man, who once described himself as looking like two sacks of manure tied together with string. Before the war he had been a schoolmaster and had written a children's book, which had had some limited success, so he had determined to make it the first of a series, using the same characters, rather like the *Famous Five* books of Enid Blyton. He settled down to this task with great industry, scribbling pages of preliminary notes and compiling an index of scenes and characters. Once, on the four-to-midnight shift, Josh came strolling round, and stood looking over Charles's shoulder for some time, eyeing the card index with approval. At last he boomed, 'Good idea, making your own traffic index – familiarises you with your traffic, helps you when you've got a garble.' The quaking indexer breathed a sigh of relief when he left without examining the cards. Whether this man ever did any decoding, or whether he left everything for the next shift, no one ever knew. He was a duplicitous character, but he had a pretty if cynical wit, and could be an amusing companion for a short time.

A very different new recruit was Charles S, an extremely tall, extremely thin flight lieutenant, with one side of his face badly scarred and his eyes always lowered. He looked at no one and spoke to no one, but sat at one of the side work surfaces with his back to the rest of the room. To the wall in front of him he pinned a large map, to which he kept up a continual soft muttering. A friend from another section came to take him to the canteen; he was led silently away, and silently returned. Mysterious stories circulated about him. He had been a pilot who had been shot down in the desert and had wandered for days without food or water. No, he had been a SIGINT man who, while carrying messages, had been captured and tortured by Tuaregs. No, his plane had crashed, killing all his crew, and he had stayed wounded in the wreckage until found. Whatever the facts, it was certain that he could not bear noises: a banging door or the scrape of a chair made him drop his head into his hands. Once a careless WAAF dropped a pile of books on to a metal table with a clang, and poor Charles S left his seat vertically, subsiding with a terrible whimpering sound. Mr B, kind man, would sometimes walk over and talk softly to him. He would lift his head and listen, seeming a little comforted by the impenetrable words and phrases. But it was evident that Charles S was not getting better, and he left one day as silently as he had come.

An equally strange but more disturbing newcomer was the wild Irish girl whom we will call Siobhan. She was the daughter of an eminent Irish senator and author, and was evidently regretting the impulse that had made her volunteer for the WAAF. As an Irish citizen she could not have been called up, and could have passed the war in perfect safety with the horses, dogs and servants among whom she had chosen to live rather than in her father's house in Dublin. Nobody could imagine how she had got through the rigid discipline of initial training. She had never been to school because she had had a governess at the family estate, and she found her present surroundings daunting and hateful. She hated England and distrusted the English, rejecting the friendly advances made by other girls. Mr B terrified her, confirming her suspicion that the British were all mad, and she would come back from the confidential little discussions on his dais (intended to help her) mouthing under her breath Irish curses, and making signs intended to avert the evil eye.

We found this out from the poet, who knew her father and had been asked to 'keep an eye' on his difficult daughter. It was like being asked to keep an eye on a wild pony. She was given a seat opposite him at the same table, and would speak to him when she would speak to no one else. His assignment was a difficult one. Siobhan learned to do some simple decoding, but for a great deal of her shift she would sit scribbling letters to her father. She wanted the poet to sit exclusively with her in the canteen, and would frowningly leave if he insisted sometimes on sitting with his friends, after which she would be furious with him for days afterwards, alternating angry silences with fishwife vituperation. The assorted grooms, servants and peasants among whom she had lived had regarded her as one of the aristocracy, and had never dreamed of correcting or criticising her behaviour, regarding it admiringly as evidence of spirit. The poet was kind and sympathetic, but she

often became enraged with his imagined neglect of her, and
once she bombarded him with everything on her table. We all
sat transfixed as the pencils, rubbers, pencil sharpeners, rulers
and other small impedimenta rolled off his head. Even Mr B
took his pipe out of his mouth. As the last crayon rolled down
his face, the poet said, as if it had just occurred to him, 'How
do you feel about playing squash tomorrow?'

Once I was on the four-to-midnight shift with her, and we
were alone in the room – the others having gone for their meal
– when Josh, roaming the block on one of his nightly rambles,
shambled in and looked over Siobhan's shoulder. Suddenly he
gave a loud shout, startling both of us. 'This WAAF', he bellowed, 'is doing unreciphered Organ!' I had never seen a piece
of unreciphered traffic and, as Siobhan had almost certainly
no idea that what she was fumbling over was called Organ, we
both stared at him uncomprehendingly. He stared back at us
through his thick lenses, expecting us to share his horror, but
I suppose we looked like two rabbits staring at a stoat. With a
kind of deep shrieking groan, he snatched up the offending
slip and lumbered from the room. We could hear his banshee
moans receding down the corridor.

But even more reluctant than our Irish colt to join the German Air Section was our token American, Sergeant Robert
Hivnor. In 1941 the Admiralty had begun to pass Intelligence from U-boat decrypts to the US Navy, who naturally
wanted to know more about the source of this information.
But it wasn't until spring 1943 that a party of American army
personnel from the US Army's Signal Intelligence Service

arrived at Bletchley to be initiated into every part of the organisation, and Bob was the unlucky man to be insinuated into Mr B's section. He was miserable at leaving his posting in the States, sad at leaving his girl and feared British stand-offishness. Most Americans were in departments where everything was clearly explained, but poor Bob came up against Mr B. Unused as he was to the English accent (for very few British films were shown in America at that time), he simply thought that he was too stupid to understand anything, so sank silently into the depths of despair. Mr B poured out reams of helpful gibberish in an attempt to cheer him up, but it was the poet who achieved this. Anxious to discuss with this new recruit the American poets he admired, Vernon Watkins soon discovered that Bob was himself a writer, mostly of plays, which his fiancée, who worked in the theatre, produced or directed; and he knew personally many poets. Bob soon became a member of our group, and we much enjoyed his dry laconic wit. He became a friend for life.

With the Americans came also Constantine FitzGibbon, who flitted only briefly across the Bletchley scene. He was very tall, very good-looking, immensely suave and the grandson or grandnephew of an Irish earl. He was regarded greedily by many a lady in F Block, but he had only recently married his handsome wife, whom everyone called Theodora even though her name was Joan – but what else could you call the wife of a Constantine? Although he was an old Harrovian, he had been staying with his American mother when war broke out, and had joined the US Army. He had a fund of comic anecdotes

illustrating the difference between English and American re-
actions. He was, for instance, flying across France in a light
aircraft when he and his pilot flew into a sea of cloud and
became lost. Through a break in the clouds Constantine suddenly recognised a landmark below. 'I know where we are,'
he exclaimed exultantly, 'we're over Rheims – there's the ca-
thedral!' His pilot, a dour man from Maine, gave him a long,
hard stare. 'Religious man?' he inquired.

The poet was later to introduce Constantine to Dylan Thomas, whose first biographer he was to become. Sadly, none of
them, though they were friends throughout their lives, was to
live into old age.

Chapter 12

Orchestra

AT THE END OF DAVID WENDT'S first year, Josh Cooper sent for him to say that he was pleased with his work and had decided to retain him in the German Air Section. Therefore he was to be discharged from the RAF to become an Air Ministry civilian employee, yet the following year he and some others were taken over by the Foreign Office. His status was unchanged, though he was now termed a junior assistant. Whatever his title, his salary was still far from princely. After deductions for billet and food, he had twenty-four shillings and nine pence to spend every week – enough for a return train ticket to London, a paperback book or a few magazines, and a few meals in a British Restaurant. David had never chosen to wear uniform, and it had tickled his fancy to be asked to sign leave applications for NCOs and officers in his capacity as head of section, while himself remaining an AC2, the lowest RAF rank of all.

At about the same time that the German Air Section moved into F Block, that other German Air organisation – the Luftwaffe – decided that they too should make some changes in their AuKa codes. They must have realised, probably as a result of monitoring by their own security service, that the RHN family of cipher keys gave the Allies a valuable recognition feature with the 'good groups'. New key sheets were introduced consisting of all the three-digit numbers from 001 to 999 in hatted (random) order, so that there were no good or bad groups. Then one of General Martini's bright young men hit upon a radical simplification in keeping with the German passion for standardisation. They had wonderfully tidy minds. There were, in addition to AuKa, a variety of low-grade codes used for such purposes as flight safety, management of radio aids such as radio beacons, fighter operations, and monitoring and jamming of Allied radar and IFF (airborne identification devices). It was decided to make the users of all these systems employ the AuKa key sheets to encipher their otherwise unrelated codes.

BP soon realised that not only were all these different codes now using three-digit keys but also that there was a relationship between recoveries from AuKa and from certain other networks. At once a combined watch was established, in which people working on each of these systems sat round a large table with a telephonist in contact with Cheadle to exchange recoveries as they were made.

A little later, the Germans thought up another 'improvement' which presented us with a range of unexpected benefits. They thought it would save paper and be much tidier if the three-digit keys were made reciprocal, and the reformed code would be simpler to use. This meant that if 012 = 234, then 234 = 012; so of course we now got two recoveries for the price of one. If we cracked cipher group 012 as meaning something which was listed in the AuKa code book with number 234, then where we found cipher group 234 in a message it must mean whatever stood opposite 012 in the code book.

But that was not all! We could apply the same process to other code systems as well! We could search traffic of the current date in all the different systems, and wherever 012 occurred we could pencil in the number 234, and vice versa. Perhaps the meaning of 234 was already known, which was likely only if we had a captured code book. If we knew the meaning in the message but had no idea of the code book number, that could now be recovered as 234. If we did not know what the group in the message meant, we now at least knew its code-book value, and could index all occurrences, past as well as future, of 234 and could compare the contexts with the hope of finding a clue as to what it meant. Previously we should have been unable to relate the occurrences, which would have remained an unrecovered key group, impossible to associate with any groups in the settings of other days.

Let us take an example. A message from an aircraft on a particular day might read '[cipher group] 012 in square [so-and-so]'. The unknown group 012 might mean 'ship' of some type or an aircraft type, or even debris or wreckage – or perhaps a rubber dinghy whose plane had been downed. Now, if the code book had been captured, we could be sure that 012 meant whatever was in the book against 234. Even if we did not possess a code book, we could assign various possible meanings to 234 and hope to establish which was correct through building up occurrences in different contexts.

In the case of AuKa, there had previously been numbers of cipher groups seen especially in convoy-sighting reports, which we could only identify tentatively as *Schiff* (ship – type unknown). Now, seeing that we had the complete code book in our hands, some of these groups could be identified with certainty, as, say, 'tanker 2000–3000 tons' or 'destroyer' or whatever, from the equation between the key group and the basic code-book number. When a key sheet was recovered from a shot-down aircraft, we could insert the basic code groups in every message. In this way we could find out the context of unusual messages which we could otherwise never have guessed. Then we were in a position to write the same meanings when similar messages cropped up again.

We could now understand the extent of the other codes, especially those in which traffic was sparse and sporadic and where the very size and scope of the code book had not been determined. If all basic code groups were found to be below, say, 150, this meant a smallish vocabulary, designed for some restricted purpose only – radar monitoring, perhaps. Where we had broken speller texts, or discovered numbers, we could now place the alphabet, and, from the span of figure groups in the code, could tell whether it catered for a full range 0–100, or only single digits or whatever. If, for example, we had guessed that, in some code system, group 012 on the day being worked meant Me-109 (a fighter aircraft), we now knew that 234 was the basic code-book number for that type. Over a period we could then determine that German aircraft types fell in the basic-code range 220–50, and could probably write in most of the types in alphabetical sequence from Arado onwards. The same process held good for many other sections of a code book laid out by our logical and tidy-minded opponents.

The name Orchestra was applied by the German Air Section to the whole complex of codes using the daily-changing AuKa three-digit key sheets. Different codes were given the names of musical instruments: Piccolo, Bassoon, Trumpet, Mandolin and the like. Another group of codes were called by the names of composers: Bach, Mozart and so on. Yet other code systems – those to do with radar and technical units – were called after noises: Bump, Clang and so on. David was once allowed to name a new code, as a reward for having discovered it. He was at home on leave, and had tuned in to a German radio station, as he often did when he had an opportunity, to keep up his knowledge of current German. A musical concert was suddenly interrupted, and a woman announcer read out a *Wasserstandsmeldung* (a water-level report). This was such a trivial subject that there could not possibly be any reason to break off a concert for its reading. To David's surprise, a male speaker read out a long string of figures, with no indication of what rivers were concerned. He grabbed paper and pencil and was able to log the complete text, since the whole message was repeated. It turned out to be a speller, a very simple substitution code, and he was able to break it without trouble. It gave advance warning of an Allied bomber stream approaching the

Ruhr. David did not think it important enough to go back to
Bletchley; he assumed that this sort of thing was already well
known and covered. But when he returned the next day, he
found that in fact it had not been picked up – it was an example of desperate improvisation on the part of the Germans.
He was invited to christen the code in the composers series,
which was to do with air defence. He would have liked to call
it Rachmaninov, but that was thought too cumbrous, so he
had to settle for Delius.

In his presence people appeared pleased, but when he was
out of the room pundits streamed in to question his head of
section and offer congratulations to be passed on to the brilliant young code-breaker. (It was so like BP to assume that
he would be embarrassed if praised in person – a very public-
school attitude!) It did not, however, occur to David that his
colleagues would think it a rather extraordinary feat. He probably assumed that most people on leave listened in to German
radio stations, and frequently heard and broke new codes. He
thought that he had done only what anyone else would have
done, had they been listening to that particular broadcast. He
really was one of Josh Cooper's bright stars.

The party handling German Luftwaffe traffic from the Russian Front had been disbanded, and David had been returned
to the main section. A change had come over the work. The
Allies had invaded France and were also driving north through
Italy. The RAF ranged over most of the remaining German-
occupied territory. In the east the Soviets rolled on relentlessly
towards the frontiers of the Reich. The Luftwaffe, struggling

against huge odds, was no longer a threat. At the end of 1944, the V-weapons, the flying bombs, the secret weapons on which Hitler based his last hopes, were hurried into action. Despite heavy attacks by our bombers, the V1 sites in the Pas de Calais launched their missiles towards London. They were actually controlled by the Luftwaffe, and BP dealt with radio messages between the sites and their regimental HQ. Using cover terms such as *Weissbrot* (white bread) and *Wepfe* (whelp), the sites reported regularly the number of bombs launched successfully, those which went out of control or were duds, and remaining stocks. Such material was supplemented by information from high-grade intercepts. As the Allies advanced to the Rhine and Holland, the V1 menace receded, although the V2 rockets continued to strike south-east England for some time. These, however, were fired not by the Luftwaffe but by German artillery troops, since they were thought of not as flying machines but missiles, like long-range shells.

David was now working on various minor codes. There were German units which monitored Allied airborne navigational and bombing radar signals, using them to track approaching formations heading for Germany, and there were other units which tried to jam these radars. The destruction of landlines through our bombing caused these units to communicate by radio in code, but what they said was almost impossible to break, consisting largely, as it did, of a stream of short messages, each giving a bearing on the target – with occasional pulse recurrence frequency – or some such technical detail. The few messages which diverged from this dreary norm were nearly always reports spelling out that the German intercept site had experienced a loss of power or that its emergency generator was now unserviceable.

This unspeakably dull traffic caused David to have a kind of brainstorm. A sudden sense of the futility of what he was doing, and a desire to do something active, impelled him to write out his resignation and send it up the pneumatic tube to the admin. office. His immediate supervisor, Flying Officer Laurie Hodges, hearing what he had done, raced to the terminal, retrieved the letter and tore it up. He told David not to be a fool, since even if his resignation were accepted, which was very unlikely, he would only end up back in Bletchley after months of square-bashing.

This swift reaction must have been the only sudden impulse that Laurie H had ever given in to. He was a very placid man, of outstandingly orderly habits, which were as predictable as his speech. It was impossible not to like him, but often you wondered why he irritated you so much. Every evening, precisely at the end of the shift, and not a moment before, he would check that his tie was correctly tied, put on his officer's hat absolutely straight (he always wore uniform, because he thought it the right thing to do), pick up his polished briefcase and say, 'Well, I shall soon be up the wooden stairs to Bedfordshire.' The poet would writhe in his chair and say, 'Laurie, I know Kierkegaard says repetition is a sacred category, but couldn't you, just once, go up the wooden stairs to some other county? Lanarkshire, say, or Merioneth?' Laurie would smile politely but uncomprehendingly at him, bow to the girls and say, like Dixon of Dock Green (who did not yet exist), 'Well, goodnight all.' He was exactly like the character in one of Ibsen's plays, who, surrounded by the bodies of people who have shot themselves and others, says in bewilderment, 'But nice people don't do such things.'

After this episode, David was given more and more miscellaneous codes to break, among which were messages about the German jamming of Allied radio broadcasts. This was evidently training of some kind. There were no organised crypt courses in those days, except for people going on missions in occupied territory. However, David was given some hints and a little assistance, and though modestly doubtful of his own ability he did well, and thus became recognised as a crypt-linguist in embryo.

Meanwhile, I in my much lower sphere had been given charge of very unimportant traffic lumped together under the name of Cymbal. It consisted mostly of small stations which seemed to be mainly concerned with the minutiae of supply and demand. There was by that time much more demand than supply in the German Air Force – in the whole of Germany, in fact, because shortages were now endemic. Since there often existed in the code book no groups for such trivialities, the greater part of this traffic consisted of spellers, which was interesting for the code-breakers. I was particularly fond of two *Feldwebeln* (sergeants), evidently quite elderly, who were friends. Perhaps they had done their training as radio operators together, or fought on the same front when they were younger, or perhaps they had even been boys in the same village. At any rate, when they were both on duty at the same time in their different stations they would get through their routine messages as quickly as possible, and then have a short gossip.

The first and greatest rule of all senders of messages in code is never, never send one group more than is necessary. (Simply sending 'Heil Hitler' at the end of a message was a great help even to the Enigma decoders.) These two would undoubtedly have been shot if they had been monitored, but the failing Reich had no manpower or time to spy on unimportant stations any longer. One of my German sergeants (call him Hansi) was fond of Mozart; the other (possibly Friedl) sometimes quoted Schiller, to which Hansi would respond by capping the quotation. *'Denkt Ihr an mich,'* Friedl might send at the end of a message; *'Ich werde Zeit genug,'* Hansi would send back. The actual quotation from Schiller is,

Denkt Ihr an mich ein Augenblickchen nur,
Ich werde Zeit genug an Euch zu denken haben.

'Think of me just for a moment,' one elderly man had sent to another in a collapsing Germany. 'I shall have enough time to think about you,' his friend had signalled back. I was very sorry for them, and I hoped that they would survive the war and live to meet again.

I was surprised one morning to find a message from Hansi among the other traffic, because he had been going on leave. It was obviously a speller, but I couldn't make anything of it. The midnight-to-eight shift had pencilled in a few kracks, among which were 'o', 'e' and 'r', so that the message looked like '-o-e-o-o----ra-e-------e--a--ro-e--o--er'.

All those 'o's worried me, especially the two close together; it could be a word made up of *ob* (whether, on account of) and some other element beginning with 'o'; but then there was a group in AuKa for *ob*. The 'er' at the end looked like German, but all those 'o's looked more like Italian to me – Italian! Hansi loved Mozart! *The Seraglio* was usually sung in German, but what about *The Marriage of Figaro*? What was the countess's aria? *'Dove sono i giuramenti / Di quel labbro menzogner?'* Poor Hansi was saying that his Oberleutnant had lied to him about his leave, and had cancelled it.

Years afterwards, in 1977, I was terribly pleased to read in *The Knox Brothers* an account of how Dilly Knox – one of BP's first great Enigma-breakers – had also come across a message in poetry while code-breaking in the First World War. He had recognised some of the three-letter groups in a message as 'en', one of the commonest endings in German. The message had looked like this:

```
-- -- -- --en -- --en -- --en
-- -- -- --en -- -- -- -- --en
```

The more Dilly looked at this pattern, the more it looked like poetry to him. In what metre? It looked like dactyls, and with the 'en' at the ends of both lines there was probably a rhyme. Any radio operator who would be quoting poetry must be sentimental, Dilly thought, and with a romantic German one of

the 'en's could be *Rosen*. He consulted some German literature experts, and they immediately identified the lines. They
were an epigram of Schiller's:

Ehret die Frauen; sie flechten und weben
Himmliche Rosen im erdliche Leben.

It gave me great pleasure to think that the most eminent and
the humblest of code-breakers sometimes faced the same kind
of problem.

Chapter 13

The Camp

AT ABOUT THE SAME TIME that Orchestra appeared, another huge upheaval took place for the members of the RAF. For some time the army had had its own camp, on the eastern side of the Park, but the Air Force camp was begun later and seemed to take a long time to complete. It was built in the fields south-west of the Park, and consisted of more than two hundred buildings. It must have cost, to use current phraseology, a bomb and a half, and was intended to relieve the pressure to find new billets ever farther and farther afield. However, whatever the costs of billets and transport for RAF personnel might have been, the costs of the camp must have outstripped them by miles. Besides living, bathing, dining and leisure quarters for the code-breakers, there had to be the same for the hundreds of people needed for the running of a huge camp: admin. officers and clerks, cooks, butchers, laundry staff, hairdressers, mechanics, electricians, equipment staff and police, to name but a few. There had, too, to be a NAAFI stores, a library and medical quarters as well as orderlies and doctors. There seemed no end to the numbers of people required to look after hundreds of other people who had, for the past three or four years, with the help of their landladies, been looking after themselves quite well.

There were also dozens and dozens of ACHs (Aircraft Hands), the lowest grade of all Air Force trades, who did all the menial jobs like cleaning the ablutions or the officers' quarters, sweeping the parade ground, taking out the rubbish and collecting the pigswill, and in fact doing any job that no one else wanted to do, for the lowest pay in the service. The BP people were indignant that a famous string quartet, which had been allowed to stay together, and had been posted to Bletchley, were now, in the camp, all grade five, since according to Air Force regulations all musicians were ACHs and were expected to do menial jobs about the camp when not practising. They also had to play selections from *The Desert Song* and *Rose Marie* when the camp commandant had visitors.

Most people did not want to leave their billets. They liked having a room to themselves, and did not relish returning to communal living in huts with thirty or so fellow humans, and to long rows of baths, washbowls and lavatories with the minimum amount of privacy. This was quite apart from turning out with towel and spongebag in underclothes and overcoats on cold winter mornings and evenings. Many of them, too, had become friends with their landladies, and knew that there would be hardship for the families or widows in losing the exiguous payments, and the extra ration book.

Ann Lavell, who was a kind of secretary or personal assistant to Josh Cooper, hated the camp, and wrote in *Station X*, 'We were hauled out of our billets, many of us wailing and screaming mightily, and . . . were put into these frightful huts that . . . had these dangerous cast-iron stoves in them that got red-hot and sent out smoke everywhere.'

Besides this, the camp personnel, especially the officers and non-commissioned officers, were intensely indignant that they could not only be refused entrance to the Park but were also not even allowed to know what went on there, or what the code-breakers (whom they considered to be under their command) did when they were inside. Of course they must have been warned about this, but probably by civilians, who they thought knew nothing about how a camp should be run; and they had quietly decided that it should be run in the usual way. But it was not a usual camp.

'There was a terrible feeling', Ann said, 'between the camp authorities and the Bletchley Park people. They couldn't bear it because they didn't know what we did, and because we could get in past the sentries . . . and some of the officers tried to bully out of the junior people what they were doing.' Foiled in this, they tried in revenge to exert their powers by ordering the camp to function in the proper way, with parades, kit inspections, floor and button polishing and every way of encroaching on free time that petty tyranny could suggest. This did not work because the code-breakers simply went into the Park, or said that they were on shift or had to sleep because they were on night shift, so that the inspections were carried out in empty huts. So few people turned up for the parades that it was impossible to drill them.

The camp officers could not complain, because the code-breakers' bosses were not available to be complained to. It was a war they could not win, so they settled down to a kind of armed neutrality, ignoring or harassing the Bletchleyites where they might have been friends. The camp sergeants and flight sergeants, many of whom were regulars, or at least had had to work for years before getting their stripes, were very puzzled by the huge numbers of BP sergeants and flight sergeants who now flooded the camp. They expected to be told, in a matey way – being all NCOs together – why the Park needed such a plethora of NCOs without any 'erks' (lower ranks) to be ordered about. They were so indignant at being kept in the dark that I believe two separate sergeants' messes had to be built.

The Park workers were also indignant that when they came back to camp after work or leave there was a sentry at the gates who said, 'Halt! Who goes there?' Some made a jocular reply, and were alarmed to see a rifle pointed at them. If, feeling idiotic and giggling, you said 'friend', you were told 'advance, friend, and be recognised', which made you giggle even more, and annoyed the sentry. One diminutive WAAF, a miniature beauty, accustomed to be treated with deference, said sharply to the sentry, 'I'm not your friend, and you don't know me, so how can you recognise me?' The guard was called out and she was taken to the guardroom, refusing to march in step with them, and telling them all the way how stupid they were.

The Officer of the Guard that night was a very young flying officer, just commissioned, and I expect he had nightmares for some time about dear little Bambi, who told him in no un-certain terms what she thought of him. She could not be put on a charge, because there was no way in which she could be released from her shift, so the incident had to be swept under the mat. The sentries faded away some time afterwards, to our great relief.

But there was one thing that the camp commandant could, and did, insist on: that we all wore uniform at all times. The old easy days of wearing civilian clothes so that you did not know, or care, whether you were speaking to a wing commander or a civilian were gone for ever. Salutes, too, were now obligatory in the camp. Most of the code-breakers had forgotten how and when to salute, and the sight of an officer's cap did not auto-matically send the arm shooting upward. This was one offence the camp officers could and did punish, since it was a matter of camp discipline. Gone, too, were the friendly lunches and dinners in the canteen; every airman and airwoman had to eat in the camp, in the sergeants' mess.

Pay parades, too, were now intensely formal occasions, run by a camp sergeant, with many bellowed orders, much stand-ing at attention and saluting. They were enlivened by the fact that the poet almost always picked up his money, saluted smartly, and marched into a broom cupboard which was next to the exit. There was a certain amount of banging and rattling, as he wrestled with mops and buckets, and then he would re-appear, smiling cheerfully, and say to the accounts officer who sat waiting impatiently at his table, 'Isn't that stupid of me? I nearly always do that, you know.' Then he would amble out, entirely forgetting the formality of the occasion. The duty sergeant would almost visibly steam with frustration, but the poet outranked him so there was nothing he could do.

However, being in camp was not all bad. There was no early rush for the transports, for one thing, and you could see something of your friends after work. You could go to the cinema in Bletchley, or stay in the Park for a concert or to watch Hugh Alexander play twenty simultaneous matches, or visit the Services club. And you did not have to drag all your luggage into the section when you were going on leave. You could put it ready packed on your bed, and just pick it up and walk genteelly down to the station.

Another pleasant thing was that in your hut you met people you had never met before, whom you would never have met if you had stayed in billets, where life was necessarily rather solitary, as it was unlikely that your friends, who were mostly those in your own section, would be living near enough to see you often. But in the hut were girls who had been unknown to you among the thousands in the Park, who now lived in that strange intimacy of a hut, where your bed was a couple of yards away from another bed on either side, and where you listened to the joys, sorrows and anxieties of other lives. A girl I grew very fond of was Vera, a twenty-four-year old Lancashire factory girl, whose life was entirely bound up with the lives of her four younger brothers and sisters, whom she had looked after ever since her mother became ill. She would work for two weeks, and then take both her days off together, so that she could make the journey north to see her family, and all her meagre pay was spent on these journeys. In the hut, she was the person you went to if you did not know how to mend something, or how to do your hair, or how to get a stain off your tunic. She became our mother, just as she was mother in her own home. We felt rather lost when she was on leave. She certainly knew no German, so she must have been a typist or stationery keeper in some block somewhere, but work was the one taboo subject in the hut. I never heard a girl ask another 'what do you do?' or 'where do you work?'

All at once an element of glamour entered our lives. A tall, very elegant girl with a slight French accent came swanning into the hut one day; she was Francine, the daughter of an air commodore and a French comtesse, and had always had a personal maid to look after her. She could not brush her own hair nor make her own bed. Vera immediately took charge of her and would see that she got to work in time every morning. (In the evenings Francine was always out, coming in just before the 23.59 deadline.) She never ate in the sergeants' mess, but was swept away by American officers in jeeps, who waited for her outside the gates.

There was high drama one day when Vera discovered a pile of underclothes behind Francine's bed – not the sturdy WAAF issue, but lovely delicate things of apricot or almond-blossom pink or primrose silk, trimmed with lace. With horror on her face, Vera told Francine that they must be washed at once; and half the hut trooped to the ablutions to see this lesson in laundry work. It was not successful. Francine would do no more than dabble her slight fingertips in the soapy water, protesting that she did not like to touch things that had been used. It ended in Vera packing a parcel every week for Francine to send home, and when the beautifully washed and folded things came back Vera would stroke them softly before putting them away. They represented romance to her.

When Francine had been in billets, her father had contrived that her maid should be billeted near her, but even an air commodore could not manage to insinuate a maid into camp. However, he did the next best thing: his daughter was spirited away to become an officer, after which she would have a bat-woman to look after her. When she left, all the glamour left the hut, too.

The men in Mr B's section, with the usual male dislike of change, had managed to get a hut together. Maurice, Denys, the poet and other cronies of theirs had taken possession of Hut Fifty-four in the RAF camp. Men were not allowed in the WAAF camp, which was stationed chastely away from the male huts, with a neutral area in between which contained buildings available to both sexes. The poet often found himself wandering inadvertently in the WAAF camp, the police quarters, the stores or the medical centre, because among his many talents a sense of direction had been left out.

Hut Fifty-four was the scene of very varied activities. Debates, discussions, gramophone recitals, games of hockey with a rolled-up sock and anything that came to hand as a stick were held in an atmosphere of friendly rivalry. Maurice regarded cynically the British love of games as demonstrating an inability to grow up, and would sit reading Dostoevsky or Hâfiz, or writing a letter in some esoteric language, looking up now and then to utter an Arabic curse as his bed was shaken. The poet caused the whole hut great anxiety, as his matutinal wanderings in search of the ablutions, and his attempts once he had washed to find his own hut again, led him far afield. The kitchen-hands stopped serving breakfast on the dot of 7.30, when he was still wandering forlornly about the camp, so the Hut Fifty-four personnel took it in turns to save for him some porridge, sausages or bacon or scrambled eggs, and some toast, which they carefully covered with another plate to keep hot. He was always grateful when he finally arrived, saying in a tone of wonder, 'Can you believe it? I actually got lost!'

They could believe it, because he got lost every evening, too, when he went to take a bath. If his absence became too pro-longed, Tim E – as the youngest member of the hut – was sent out, grumbling, on reconnaissance. If he became diverted by a newspaper in the library or a glass of cider in the NAAFI, a search party would sally forth, so that when at last the lost one arrived he would find the hut empty. These peregrinations, however, and the hassle attendant on them, did not discon-cert the poet in any way. He was in bliss. Hitherto he had, by scouring F Block or even in desperation the whole Park, found people to play tennis or squash with him occasionally, but now actually in the hut itself, almost unnoticed in a corner bed, was a young man (confusingly called Dennis) who had played table tennis for his county. Then began a contest more bitterly fought than Wimbledon or the World Cup, but always with good temper and enjoyment. The opponents were about as good as each other: Dennis had the better technique; the poet more determination. They would play until they were exhausted or until the crowd waiting their turn at the table became too vociferous to be ignored. They played at lunch time too, having gobbled their meal at top speed, and the poet's return to his section became later and later, until even long-suffering Mr B made some mild expostulation.

The poet, unlike the rest of us, felt sorry for the camp NCOs and was on civil terms with one of them, who complained bitterly that the code-breakers' huts, which were supposed to be in his charge, were in a disgraceful state. In a sudden spirit of co-operation the poet decided to polish his floor space, hoping to stimulate his hut mates to clean or at least tidy their spaces. On a day when he did not have to be on shift until four o'clock, he supplied himself from the cleaning cupboard at the end of the hut with broom, polishing mop and tin of polish. He tied a duster over the broom and spread the polish rather thickly, then began with enthusiasm to rub the polishing mop over it. To his dismay, the floor – instead of gleaming like a mirror – became duller and duller the more he rubbed. A colleague, waking at the other end of the hut and coming nearer to inspect this unusual activity, pointed out that the tin he had picked from the cupboard contained dubbin not floor polish.

A late recruit to the section and to Hut Fifty-four was Lewis R, the son of a well-to-do Scottish businessman. He was a tall, bespectacled young man, very urbane and cultured, devoted to good writing and good conversation. His taste in literature was well in advance of the current fancy. If Lewis was reading some author unknown to you, you could be sure that soon that author would be among the most discussed by the literati of the time. Cigarettes of a special Turkish brand, exquisitely but faintly scented, called Sub Rosas, were sent to him regularly by the carton. He said that at his previous station, where he had been a photographer, his impoverished colleagues would lurk outside his hut window, to retrieve the rejects which he discarded as being squashed or crumpled in packing. He was a delightful person, for all his rather aloof, eighteenth-century demeanour – one could imagine him, and his friend David too, being carried to the guillotine in a tumbril with the same unmoved expressions, flicking specks of dust from the lace at their wrists.

By now the tide of the war was beginning to turn in the Allies' favour. The British and American armies linked up in North Africa, and a complete picture of Rommel's plans was being forwarded by BP to the commanders. Although the lowly code-breakers in the German Air Section were ignorant that Ultra composed the bulk of Germany's top-secret communications – ignorant indeed that there was such a thing as an Enigma machine – still, the mood at BP was hopeful now. People had always tried to be cheerful and to keep each other's spirits up, but now there was a real reason for looking towards a possible end to the war. The U-boat menace had been overcome. By May 1943 Admiral Doenitz had called off his 'wolf packs' from the Atlantic, which meant that supplies could be brought to Britain in preparation for the invasion of Europe, which everyone knew would take place some time in the next year.

Although some people hated all of the camp all of the time, I didn't. I missed dear Mrs Henson, but found my hut quite cosy, and it was certainly pleasant to be able to have a bath again instead of a Victorian sponge-down. Then, too, I made friends with people I would never otherwise have met. But, with hindsight, the camp was an expensive mistake. Of course it had taken years to build, and the Air Ministry could not at that time guess that the war would end when it did. In fact the camp was closed less than two years after it opened. If you go to Church Green Road now, you will find no trace of all that bustling life, all those cheerful, arguing, shouting, singing voices are silent, and nothing exists to show that they were ever there.

Chapter 14

The End of the Park

As the Americans and British advanced towards the Rhine, and the Russians raced for Berlin, BP ceased to have much effect on the Allied progress. It did, however, help in Operation Crossbow, the plan to counter the last efforts of the Germans to bombard London with V-bombs. Many German Luftwaffe stations had now been overrun. In the confusion people had no time to look up their code books, and often sent their messages in 'clear' (plain language). We sometimes thought wistfully of the days when the Germans, realising that the mere fact the ground controller of a bomber crew was on the air would alert interceptors to impending operations, used to operate their net at irregular times and pass 'spoof' messages, simulating real ones. The tidy-minded Germans, however, anxious that the recipients should not be deluded into thinking this real traffic, often spelled out 'filler message', to make sure they were recognised as dummies. Operators had no time now, and often no equipment, to send even pretend traffic.

In these last months of the German Air Section, David Wendt had some consolation. Josh Cooper had actually 'enwised' him, had initiated him into the holy of holies – the restricted group who knew about Enigma. Most people in the Park not only were ignorant of anything to do with machine ciphers but also had never envisaged the possibility that, if such things existed, they could be broken. Josh now encouraged David to go to the room where Enigma decrypts were held and browse, to acquire background for his own humbler work. As German Air traffic dwindled, there was of course plenty of time for this.

David found the material fascinating. It immensely expanded his knowledge of German military terminology, procedure and organisation. (This was later to be invaluable in his postwar work for the Control Commission in Germany.) He was able to glance through some messages dealing with the German struggle with the partisans in Yugoslavia. Through this, it became apparent from a German casualty return after one battle, in which Tito's Communist partisans had been bloodily defeated, that the Serbian Chetniks under Mihailovich were, at that time at least, fighting as allies of the Germans against Tito. Other messages referred to an 'SS Brigade Handschar' (*hancar* is a Turkish word for 'dagger'), and this unit was further described as Bosnian Moslem. No doubt it took part with enthusiasm in the war against the partisans. David, much later, was well able to understand the complex hatreds which still bedevil the Balkans. The Serb detestation of the Muslims goes back to the centuries when most of south-eastern Europe up to the Austrian border was under Turkish rule. Even a hundred or so years ago Turkish Bashi-Basouks (what would now be called militia) were inflicting hideous massacres on their Christian neighbours.

He also grew familiar with the geography of central and eastern Europe. He was interested to find that many places had three or four different names, because they had been occupied at various times by diverse nations. He found a map of Yugoslavia published in Vienna soon after the end of the First World War, when the country had been created from the former Austrian possessions of Croatia and Slovenia, together with Serbia, Bosnia-Herzegovina and Montenegro. What the German-speaking Austrians had called, for example, Gross Betschkerek, the Hungarians named Nagy Betskerek and the Serbs Veliki Beckerek. It was the same in Transylvania, now part of Rumania. The area had been colonised in the Middle Ages by German Saxons and by Hungarians. One town was Cluj to the Rumanians, Koloszvar to the Magyar Hungarians and Klausenberg to the Germans. In the Baltic area, what was Pskov to the Russians was Picskau to the Germans and Pcipus to the Estonians.

In these browsings among the Enigma decrypts, David saw glimpses of the war situation from the other side. Many of the messages were on routine subjects, but among them were decrypts of reports from concentration camps to the RSHA (the headquarters of Himmler's SS and police empire). He was left in no doubt of the truth of the Holocaust rumours. Years before, when he was still at Cambridge, a young Jewish student had told him that the Germans were exterminating Jews in Poland and were beginning a systematic genocide in other countries. He had refused to believe that any race could be so barbarous, or so insensitive to world opinion. He knew better now. Walter Eytan, who had been born in Germany and was Jewish, recalled a similar but for him even more poignant moment in late 1943, or early 1944, when the Z Watch in Hut Four intercepted a signal from a German ship taking Jews to Piraeus in Greece *zur Endloesung* (towards the final solution). There was no need for him to wonder what that 'solution' might be. It was a moment that he remembered all his life.

Strangely, during this period when air traffic was diminishing, a last feeble influx of newcomers flowed into the Park. Perhaps they were intercept operators who had to be put somewhere to await demobilisation while their stations were closed down; perhaps the professional code-breakers were trying to build up empires, so as to ensure high status when they returned to civilian life in what had been GC&CS (known to those who did not admire it as the Golf, Chess and Crossword Society) but was henceforth to be GCHQ (Government Communications Headquarters). This organisation was to move first to Eastcote in Middlesex and then to its permanent home in Cheltenham.

Mr B's watch was to have only one girl from this trickle of newcomers, but she was to bring about his downfall. She was a Scottish girl in her late twenties, called Betty. Whatever her trade in the Air Force had been, it was impossible to think of her as anything but a children's nanny of the very best type.

She made no attempt to learn anything about decoding, and indeed there was not much traffic coming into the section by now. Betty took over the room and Mr B, not to speak of the rest of us, as though it were a children's nursery. He had always left his mug filled with tea overnight, and would drink the nauseating cold mixture with relish as soon as he sat at his table in the morning. Betty soon put a stop to this. She collected all mugs after the afternoon tea round, took them to the washroom and returned them – clean and shining and free from the tannin stains of years – to the owners. Mr B protested weakly at first, but she dismissed his complaints kindly but firmly, telling him how unhygienic the practice was and what frightful infections he might catch. 'And I dinna trust that nasty dried milk neether,' she said. She would remove his pipe gently from his mouth as he sat sucking it contentedly, while we all held our breath. 'Ye're rrrruining your lungs,' she said. 'What you need is guid fresh air,' and she would fling the window open, crying 'it's awfu' stuffy in here anyway!' 'I dinna ken whit you're on aboot,' she would tell him, picking up his papers and stacking them neatly in the wrong piles. 'Noo tek it nice and slow and mebbe I'll get ye.' Poor Mr B! He was a broken man. No rage, no protests could dim her unchanging patience and good temper. He would excitedly tell George T about the wrongs and indignities he suffered at her hands, and George would nod and smile pleasantly. Mr B's own smiles, once so rapid and brilliant, were now mere shadows of themselves, wan and feeble.

Betty would also go round tables with a duster – Heaven knows where she had picked it up. She would tidy all the scattered paraphernalia of office life, so that their owners looked in vain for objects that had been in the same place for years. She would empty all the waste-paper baskets into one, in spite of Denys's agonised cries of 'Betty! that's Secret Waste – nobody's supposed to touch that!' 'Oh, pish-tush,' she would say good-humouredly, 'am I no juist helpin' the cleaners?' She was a dear girl, and no one had the least idea what she was doing at Bletchley.

Soon after VE-Day, Betty disappeared, under the strange Service rule of last in, first out. Other people were vanishing too: some on compassionate grounds, some because their civilian jobs were urgently waiting for them, while others were made redundant, which meant a week's pay and out. The German Air Section was wound up, and the Air Force personnel who were awaiting demobilisation, together with those code-breakers who intended to stay on as professionals, were deployed 'down the Burma Road' and sent to the Japanese Air Section at the other end of the corridor.

In the Japanese Section, David spent some months poring over a dreadful system which seemed expressly designed to send the user blind. He had to scan the top line of a square of digits, pick out the one required, drop the eyes down the column to find another digit, then swivel his eyes to the left margin to obtain the resultant digit. He needed to rest his eyes often, but, even so, doing it for hours left him giddy and sick.

After VE-Day Henry 'Pope' Dryden was transferred to the Air Section to train staff as they became available from other sections for work in the Japanese Air Section. This changed from having less than two hundred decoders to more than seven hundred, drawn from all ranks of all the Services. After VJ-Day (15 August 1945) there was a gradual reversal of this process during which this big breezy army major was continually being harassed by telephone calls asking how many lampshades, and of what size, were on his property sheets, as well as other such completely irrelevant matters. Meanwhile David to his great relief was made redundant. I had left some months before, in May.

Barbara Abernethy of the Civil Service and an army colonel were the last two left at Bletchley Park. They closed all the huts and blocks, put some files in cartons to go to Eastcote and then the colonel left. Barbara was alone in the Park, where such a short time ago there had been no single day or night when it was not crowded with workers. All the voices which had sounded in it, laughing, complaining, discussing, arguing, explaining, grieving were silent now. She locked the gates through which so many thousands had passed, and turned away.

Writing of the end of BP inevitably brings to my mind the German Air Section's 'onlie begetter', that great man whose mind was throughout the war set on the saving of Britain and the defeat of the Nazis, J. E. S. Cooper. I never knew him personally, only as the much admired and half-feared head of the department. David knew him as a friend, so he should be the one to speak of the Josh he knew.

Of the many people at BP, such as Alan Turing, who later became famous for their leading part in the solution of

Enigma and other feats, I had no knowledge at the time. Then, the need-to-know principle was strictly applied, and one was only aware of this or that distinct personality – trim or dishevelled, weird or nondescript – among the crowd, without having any inkling of what each did. Thus I can only discuss in any detail the few figures who featured in the closed compartment in which I worked. And among those by far the most interesting was Josh Cooper. He was outstanding in his eccentricity and also because of his many-sided knowledge and experience.

My first impression of Josh Cooper, when I went to Bletchley and was interviewed by him in the hut at the gate, was of a broad, solidly built man, of middle age, with lank dark hair and a pallid, heavy-featured face. As he grew more familiar later on, he became a distinct individual, taller than I had originally thought, somewhat bulky. His stance was upright, his gait rather measured, stiff and a bit splay-footed. His manner was polite, and his speech educated upper-class English. We were all on first-name terms. Josh I remember usually wore rather baggy and well-worn clothes – a dark suit as a rule.

Later on I was privileged to attend some talks Josh gave to members of the Air Section who had been 'enwised' but not told details of the manner in which Enigma and similar systems had been solved. I was struck by his grasp of those extraordinary processes, and his ability to convey them in outline to less talented minds. But what struck me especially was his wide familiarity with many languages. This was an area in which I could follow his explanations readily, and they stimulated my interest in comparative linguistics – not that I ever attained more than a superficial acquaintance, based on smatterings of a number of tongues. I never could emulate Josh's depth of erudition.

Josh seemed to spend most of his time, when not engaged in some specific task, revolving other themes in his head, and he hated waste of time. One day in 1948, after my return to GCHQ, I was working alone in a small office when . . . Josh came in. 'Give me something to read, will you?' he said. 'Anything at all will do. I have ten minutes before the meeting.' This was a poser. My cupboard held no books or interesting reports of any kind, merely worksheets and the like; no printed literature, not even a dictionary. I grabbed a folder, not knowing what it contained, and gave it to him. He sat down heavily and immersed himself in the contents, while I resumed my work. After a while, Josh rose, handed me back the folder with a word of thanks and walked out.

In considering Josh Cooper's many skills, we should not forget that he was a gifted talent spotter and was charged with picking likely recruits. Josh . . . rated my German as not up to the required standard for BP but by inquiring into my hobbies and interests he elicited my dabblings in oriental languages and established that I was able to memorise Japanese kana as well as some Chinese characters.

The poet, who had a curious faculty for spotting plain 'goodness' in other people, also had a great reverence for and devotion to Josh. If he heard that Josh was patrolling the corridor, he would dart out of the section, catch him up and walk alongside him, talking confidentially and with great enjoyment. What on earth did they talk about, these two who were probably the most eccentric men in F Block? Mr B had been behind them in one of these jaunts and said to the poet afterwards, 'I heard you say "Sir" just now. Why don't you call him "Josh"?' 'Oh, I couldn't,' replied the poet earnestly, 'it would be like saying to God, "Hey there, Jehovah".'

We all laughed over tales of Josh's eccentricities, but I think there was not one of us who did not realise that that massive brain had no attention to spare for the minutiae of daily life because it was solely concentrated on its one task of helping to save civilisation. If the Germans had conquered Britain, the lights would indeed have gone out all over Europe. It was no surprise to us to read in *The Hut Six Story* that after the war Josh had confessed to Gordon Welchman that his work at BP had been an almost intolerable strain, because 'success so often depended on flashes of inspiration for which he would be searching day and night, with the clock always running against him.' The *Dictionary of National Biography* refers to 'the great range of his mind and his ability to comprehend in fields such as mathematics and physics which were outside those in which he had been educated' and 'his extraordinary memory and instant recall'. It states too that he 'was always admired and beloved by those who worked for him'. He was indeed.

To work in BP had been an unforgettable experience. Josh
Cooper had said that a stint there should count as a university
degree. In fact it was much more. In no university had there
ever been so many extraordinary people gathered together;
no modern think-tank or high-level conference could approach it. Everyone there was dedicated to one end – decoding and extracting for use every scrap of information from
the enemy's codes. Almost everyone at BP – of those over
twenty years old at least – was also an expert in some subject:
mathematics, history, languages and literature ancient and
modern, literary history and criticism, music, chess, papyrol-
ogy and epigraphy, theology, politics, geography – you name
it, BP had it. If the knowledge in the brains of BP could have
been extracted, it would most certainly have filled volumes
and volumes of encyclopaedias.

Words cannot express the combined brilliance of the BP
world. Perhaps if all its personnel had been kept together after
the war to consider the problems of world peace and universal
prosperity, they might have cracked those problems too. Many
people there regarded it as the zenith of their lives. For example,
Edward Thomas, the naval officer who had boarded the U-570
to discover the box which showed BP that the Germans were
using a fourth rotor for their U-boat signals, said of his arrival
in Hut Three, 'We naval newcomers were at once impressed by
the easy relations and lack of friction . . . A spirit of relaxation
prevailed. Anyone of whatever rank or degree could approach
anyone else, however venerable, with any idea or suggestion,
however crazy.' 'It was out of this world,' commented Ann

Lavell, Josh's secretary. Gordon Welchman wrote that 'BP . . . was a very happy place to live and work. Many of us look back to BP days as the best period of our lives.' Hugh Denham (of the Japanese Naval Section, in Hut Seven) suggested that the most important thing to record was 'the priceless sense of community that formed. We were in our teens or twenties, thrown together . . . working to a common purpose, sharing unusual experiences. The bonds that then grew have lasted.'

The Americans, too, who had perhaps been fearing the British stand-offishness, were enthusiastic. Telford Taylor, of the US Intelligence Service, commented that 'BP was certainly the end of feeling lonely. I cannot adequately portray the warmth and patience of the Hut Three denizens.' Jim Rose and Peter Calvocoressi remained close friends of his all his life. William Bundy, later to become US Secretary of State, said that it had been 'a terrific human experience and I've never matched it since. Certainly for me personally it was the high point.' Stuart Milner-Barry, one of the Hut Six decoders, wrote, 'I felt at the time – and looking back on it after more than half a century I feel the same – that I was extraordinarily lucky to have found myself in that particular job at that time . . . We were slightly ashamed, or at any rate unhappy, that we should be leading such relatively safe and comfortable lives when a large proportion of the population, whether civilian or in uniform, was in such danger. But at the same time, we could not help realising that our work . . . was of enormous importance in the conduct of the war. For that reason alone, there was a spirit of camaraderie which I think never failed us.'

(In view of these words from people who really were at BP, it is rather surprising that Robert Harris, in *Enigma*, should choose to portray BP as such a mean place, full of back-biting, back-stabbing and unpleasantness. Perhaps it is difficult for modern writers, used to the continual quarrels and vituperation of *Coronation Street* and *EastEnders*, to understand that it really was possible to work with other people day after day, even under conditions of stress, without losing one's temper or quarrelling or resorting to violence. Yet it was. Harris's hero was glad to see the back of the Park at the end of the book; and without doubt BP would have been glad to see the back of such a mean-spirited and traitorous person.)

For David Wendt and me the BP years had been an extraordinary time. We had come to BP as young, inexperienced, unfledged people and had grown up in that unbelievable atmosphere where brilliant conversation and contact with people we could never have hoped to meet in any other place had been daily occurrences. It had been, in one sense, the time of our lives. But it was over.

Chapter 15

Afterwards

YES, IT WAS OVER – all, all over. Dear Josh Cooper, who had first learned code-breaking from Ernst Fetterlein in 1925, went on to Eastcote, where David and his wife once saw him swooping out of the gates on a new motorcycle. On seeing them, he lifted both hands from the handlebars and waved a cheery greeting as the vehicle swerved wildly over the fortunately empty road. He was a great and good man.

Alan Turing, brilliant mathematician, unique genius, was given an OBE for his work at Bletchley, and continued his research into computers. In 1952 he was tried for homosexuality, then a criminal act, and his security clearance was taken away so that he could not go on with his work. He died mysteriously in 1954, possibly by his own hand. He was born, like so many geniuses, before his time. Gordon Welchman, too, suffered greatly. After the publication of *The Hut Six Story,* for which he had apparently received permission from the government but not from GCHQ, his security clearance too was taken away. He was threatened with prosecution, and possibly only his death in 1985 prevented this threat from being carried out. Stuart Milner-Barry thought he had been 'ridiculously persecuted' for telling how the Enigma codes had been broken, even forty years after. But I do not think that that was the reason for the way he was treated. I believe it was because he had revealed some of the crucial mistakes made on the reception of some vital messages. The Intelligence Service has always disliked the revelation of its shortcomings.

The dons went back to their universities, the teachers to their schools, and anyone else with a job waiting for him hurried back to it. Mr B fled thankfully from the frightful memory of Betty back to his inspectorate of schools in the Lake District. I understood exactly why he had been so early promoted from teaching, and often thought with pity of the crowds of bewildered young teachers bobbing in his wake as he cruised on his benignant way, dispensing kind, fatherly and utterly incomprehensible advice.

In October 1944, I had married our poet – Vernon Watkins. This caused a furore in the upper ranks of the camp, since it appeared that no Service man or woman could marry without the permission of the commanding officer. On being summoned to the august presence, the poet simply said, 'Well, sir, I really don't see what business it is of yours when and whom I marry.' He was always one to go straight to the point, and after all, as he also pointed out, nobody could unmarry us, so the whole matter died down. After the war, we settled on the cliffs of the glorious Gower Peninsula, the first area of Outstanding

Natural Beauty in Britain. There we brought up five children, whom Vernon dearly loved, though he would occasionally say, 'If you had only had five more, I should have had my own cricket team.' He died, like his great friend Dylan Thomas, in America, full of honours, and probably to be the next poet laureate. I cannot help feeling that, for one who all his life had loved games, it was fitting to fall dead after making the winning stroke in a tennis match of men's doubles. Vernon, Dylan Thomas and Constantine FitzGibbon were three great friends, none of whom lived to be old.

Not long after the end of the war, we called on Maurice Zarb in the Crédit Lyonnais in Threadneedle Street, London. When asked, Maurice had simply said that he worked in a bank, so we thought we might have to ask the manager whether we could see him for a moment. Instead, we were escorted by a series of deferential secretaries to an immense, expensively carpeted room, where Maurice, in a perfectly cut Savile Row suit, sat dictating to a yet more elegant secretary. But he was the same kind unassuming person, still urging us to learn Russian so that we could read Dostoevsky in the original, still dismissing the current bestsellers as of no account, but now able to see his mother in Cairo and his half-brothers and sisters all over the world.

Vernon met one of these in Paris, and was invited to coffee. Expecting to go to an *appartement*, he was driven to an exquisite small chateau outside the city, furnished with satin divans, silk and velvet cushions and ivory tables. They were waited on by doe-eyed houris bearing silver trays of thick sugared coffee and exotic sweets. This was Maurice's real background, though he had never uttered a word of complaint in the spartan BP conditions. He remained a lifelong friend, always interested in the poet's work, and deigning to express a few words of commendation about the plays of Eugène Ionescu and Samuel Beckett – always well in advance of public acclaim for these authors.

Francine married a French comte after the war, and took her rightful place in his château and his Paris *hôtel*. Those of us who remembered her in the hut would smile reminiscently when we saw her photograph in *Vogue* and *Paris Match*, looking every inch the comtesse – tall, slender and always exquisitely dressed.

David Wendt had an extraordinary time after the war. On leaving BP, he applied to join the Indian Civil Service, which was advertising for officers, since he felt that he would like to revisit the land of his birth. He was told that instead of formal examinations a selection board would be held, on the lines of the 'Country House Party' procedure used during the war to pick candidates for military commissions.

While waiting for the board, he enrolled at the London School of Oriental Languages for courses in Arabic and Turkish. He learned a fair amount in the Turkish class, but the other soon degenerated into farcical chaos, because almost all the students were American Service men and women waiting to be demobilised, and they did nothing but chat and reminisce about their wartime experiences. David also worked in Whitehall, where there was a shortage of civil servants, and was assigned to the Burma Office. Burma had been conquered by the Japanese in 1942, and since this occupation had been cruelly exploited and oppressed. As a result the Burmese elements led by Aung San and his Burma Liberation Army, who initially had welcomed the Japanese as liberators from alien British rule, turned against the Japanese when the tide of war allowed. The country was largely devastated, short of food and every kind of equipment. The British army set up a military administration, and set about restoring order from chaos. In London, the dozen or so officers in the Burma Office, most with experience of pre-war Burma, planned and organised shipments of food and supplies. They found that there were unexpected snags. For instance, while agricultural implements were desperately needed to restore rice production, it appeared that the Burmese cultivators were used to a tool called a mamootie, and would not accept any substitute. So thousands of mamooties had to be conjured up somehow.

There was one area in which David could do useful and congenial work. Apart from a few elderly and no longer very influential politicians, Whitehall had little knowledge of the political forces now coming to the fore in a Burma which would inevitably seek independence. He started a card index of personalities, using articles from the Rangoon English-language press, and other sources. There was a welter of General Councils of Buddhist Associations, rather like YMCAs (Young Men's Christian Association) with political overtones, with very restricted local influence, and mostly referred to by the names of their founders. His card index was to help those who had some knowledge of pre-war Burma to restore order after the Japanese had been defeated.

David's great difficulty was with the Burmese name system. There was a limited number of names anyway, and the same man might be referred to as U Maung, Thakin Maung, Ko Maung or Maung Maung, according to whether he was being called Mr, Lord, Comrade or Brother. There were several politicians called U Mya, differentiated only by their place of residence: U Mya Henzada, U Mya Pyawbwe and the like. He also had access to some interesting old files about frontier disputes with China, and greatly relished the translation of a memorandum to the Tsungli Yamen (the old Chinese Imperial Foreign Office), which included the following passage, 'As for the Wild Wa, ravening together like deer or swine, knowing nothing of Majesty or Glory . . .'

David was appointed to the Indian Civil Service just in time to be axed when no more expatriate officers were to be recruited, because it became clear that India would soon achieve independence. But he received a year's salary in lieu of career. There were, however, jobs being advertised in Intelligence in the British Element of the CCG (Control Commission for Germany). He was given a job on the strength of a war spent in an environment to do with Intelligence, but about which he could give no details at all! Then he returned to England and the 'ivory tower' of GCHQ, where he worked under Hugh Alexander till 1963.

It was during these years that he and his wife and two small boys would visit us in our cliff-top home, scrambling down to the then-unpeopled bays, and often talking about our Bletch-ley friends. Yet we never, never mentioned the work we had done. The silence of BP still held. We had never talked about our work during the war, and we never talked about it after-wards – not to parents, spouses, siblings or friends, who had no idea (and often died without having any idea) of what their loved ones had done during the war. The idea of permanent silence had been so branded into us that we felt we should carry it to our graves.

Dr Daniel Jones, who was then a well-known composer, re-marked to me towards the end of his life, 'I have never said a word about what went on at Bletchley Park, and I never will.' And he never did, although his wife had worked there too. Even husbands and wives who had both been there never spoke to each other about their work. It was as though it had never existed.

Commander Edward (Jumbo) Travis, who was not himself a code-breaker but the government's main adviser on codes and ciphers, became the nearest the democratic, egalitarian Park had to a head or director. On VE-Day he issued a Special Order to everyone in BP. After thanking for their hard work and loyalty, the order continued,

I cannot stress too strongly the necessity for the main-tenance of security. While we were fighting Germany it was vital that the enemy should never know of our activ-ities here . . . At some future time we may be called upon to use the same methods. It is therefore as vital as ever not to relax from the high standard of security that we have hitherto maintained. The temptation now to 'own up' to our friends and families as to what our work has been is a very real and natural one. It must be resisted absolutely.

And I believe it always was. Parents never knew what their children had done in the war, and vice versa. Even the announcement by the British government in the eighties that the former code-breakers who had worked on Enigma were now released from restrictions on discussing their work made no difference to most of us, even to those who had known nothing about Enigma.

Neil Ascherson, in an article in the *Observer* in March 1999, commented that the silence was 'as staggering as the feats of Turing and Welchman . . . Everyone who worked there was sworn to utter, permanent secrecy about what they were doing, and the oath was not lifted even when the war ended.' His sister worked as a Wren at BP, and never told her family what she had done, not even her father, a naval officer who died without knowing anything about his daughter's war. 'That silence was very British,' Ascherson wrote, 'nobody else could have kept it, and nobody was rewarded for keeping it . . . We would not be able to keep such silence today.' Of course, there were many American and code-breakers of other nationalities who presumably also kept silent.

There were survivors who even at the millennium refused to speak about what they had done. They had promised silence, and they had kept their word. But even that is not the real silence of BP. No; the real silence is the silence of all those who once worked, walked and talked in that extraordinary place – for most of them the silence of the grave. F Block has been razed to the ground. BP is now a kind of theme park. Where once we heard talk such as we shall never hear again – brilliant, witty, sparkling and always memorable – now, for us who went there when we were young, there is silence.

Remembering

J. E. S. Cooper
Irene Beane
Lyndon Bennett
Constantine FitzGibbon
Dennis Costigan
Ted Downing
Ernst Fetterlein
Paul Fetterlein
Robert Hivnor
Laurie Hodges
Daniel Jones
Eleanor Macdowall
Stephen Usherwood
Vernon Watkins
Maurice Zarb

I loved the fond, the faithful and the true.
John Clare

The days when I frequented that corner can never fade in my remembrance. I never see it and I never wish to see it now; I have been there only once since, but in my memory there is a mournful glory shining on the place, which will shine for ever.

Charles Dickens

Appendices

Appendix 1

Brief Introduction to Codes and Ciphers
by David Wendt

ALMOST WITHOUT EXCEPTION, books about the work done at Bletchley Park contain explanations and demonstrations of various codes and workings of Enigma machines of the most hideous complexity. The eye of the ordinary reader simply recoils from the appalling diagrams and patterns, and the mind becomes blank when confronted with sentences such as 'a flat-random sequence is one in which the probabilities of the "letters" of the "alphabet" are all 1/A when "t" is the size of the alphabet' or 'the teleprinter start signal of +80v changes the polarised relay to dot.' Every explanation in this book has been made as simple as possible. Any reader who wishes to make his own code book and key sheet will find it easy to do so. But then this book is, thankfully, not about the Enigma codes. One reviewer of a book about Enigma, himself a codebreaker, remarked on what many readers must much more strongly have realised, that 'parts of this book will be above the heads of many readers, as they are above mine.' Yet Gordon

Welchman, brilliant mathematician, said it would have been easy for him to be told everything he needed to know about the Enigma machine in half an hour. 'Oh!' as Dylan Thomas said of a complicated construction toy in his Christmas stocking, 'oh, easy for Leonardo!'

Nevertheless, because this book is about Bletchley Park and people employed in the Air Section there during the Second World War, we must briefly mention codes and ciphers. For those readers who are not familiar with them, we must make clear what we are talking about. A code is a way of disguising the meaning of something you want to keep secret. One way of doing this is to make your message look different from ordinary language. A scrambler phone disguises speech. But a code can also be innocent of any desire to maintain secrecy. Semaphore is an example in which two flags, held at different angles singly or in combination to represent letters of the alphabet, can spell out a message to a recipient within visual range. Similarly, Morse code uses combinations of dots and dashes to represent letters for transmission by radio or other means. Both these are now well known and do not provide secrecy. So those who want their correspondence to remain secret have to take a further step and encode their message before sending it whether by post, radio or other means.

We should remember that a code can also have innocent uses for facilitating civil communications. The Morse code made it possible for people far away from each other to exchange messages by telegraph. Then there is the international Q-code. This is a system of three-letter code groups, all beginning 'Q', each with a meaning applicable to various aspects of travel by air or sea, including weather and radio communications details. It is easily learned and suitable for exchanges of information between people contacting each other by radio, whether amateurs or professionals, like ship's radio officers or radio operators aboard an aircraft, in contact with base or with other vessels or aircraft. Thus QAA = expect to arrive at . . . ; QAB = bound for; QAL = landing; QAM = meteorological report; QST = use radiotelephony. It is easy to learn by heart and universally used. Q-code is not intended to provide secrecy but brevity, and it is meant to be intelligible to speakers of any language.

The Chinese written language is itself to non-speakers like a secret code, consisting of several thousand 'characters', each written in the same-sized square space whether it consists of a single stroke or of a complicated jumble involving more than twenty strokes. Each character has a meaning and a mono-syllabic sound, although the sound may vary widely between official Mandarin and dialects spoken in remote areas. Many of the same characters are used in Japan, where they are pronounced differently again. In order to transmit Chinese characters by telegraph, they have to be converted (encoded) – using the Chinese Telegraph Code – into four-figure groups, which the recipient can convert back into characters which he can read, provided he has a copy of the book.

A secret code has to be pre-arranged with those for whom it is intended, so that they can recognise messages and know how to read them. The code can substitute different letters for those of the message text or it can transpose them so that they look like gobbledegook. Alternatively, it can turn the letters and numbers of the text into groups of figures or letters from a list in the possession of both sender and receiver. This process is best accomplished by making up a book in alphabetical order like a dictionary, containing both single words and whole phrases in alphabetical order, so that the sender can easily find the items he wants to make up his message. But if we simply use a sort of custom-built dictionary, with a vocabulary limited to those words, numbers and so on likely to be used, the alphabetical sequence may be a giveaway to hostile parties into whose hands the message may fall.

A transposition code takes the message text and writes it out in a sequence laid down and agreed in advance. Various methods have been devised, and the German forces employed the Playfair system of a five by five square in which the alphabet (omitting 'J') is inscribed in some prearranged manner. The message is extracted by taking opposite corners of the rectangle in which each pair of letters in the plain text occur, and using adjacent letters when the plain text pair are in line vertically or horizontally.

A cipher usually transforms the text in some elaborate way, and to this type of cipher belong Enigma and other machine ciphers used by the Germans. The details of these ciphers and the way in which they were broken by the Allies during the war are beyond the scope of this book, which deals with those engaged in breaking lower-grade communications intended to provide only limited security.

To increase the security of a simple code, it can be enciphered in various ways. One method is to apply an additive. Each party is provided with both the basic code book, with which to turn plain text into groups of figures, and a book consisting of a long series of figure groups of a given length, often five-figure. These groups are ideally produced mechanically in random ways which avoid repetitions. The code groups of the encoded message are written by the sender under the additive groups, starting at some point on the page arranged in advance or indicated by some means, perhaps in the message preamble. Then the upper and lower figures are added together, without carrying. Thus the message has been changed completely to all appearance, and in theory nobody who does not have the right additive book and starting-point can work out the underlying text. The recipient, knowing the agreed starting-point, writes the reciphered text under the numbers in his identical copy of the additive book and subtracts the lower from the upper digits to arrive at the clear code groups, which he can look up in the code book of which he also has a copy.

German Air Force Low-Grade Codes

To help the reader follow references in this book, we now discuss a series of German Air Force codes ranging from a small book of a couple of pages designed for a particular set of circumstances, and used without recipherment for a brief campaign, through to a larger code book designed for use over a lengthy period in more than one area. We will see how this system developed over a period, and how more and more frequent changes of recipherment made code-breaking harder. We will also see how this elaboration ultimately took a turn which made the task of code-breaking more urgent and on the face of it more difficult, but which in fact turned out to confer great benefits on the BP code-breakers.

When I joined BP at the end of June 1942 the war in Russia was in progress, and the Luftwaffe, having lost the Battle of Britain had scaled back its raids on the UK. Meanwhile the North African campaign was being fought, with varying fortunes. The Luftwaffe bomber units in all theatres were now using air–ground codes with three-letter encipherment of the basic table, changing monthly. The name RHN was given by us to the series of codes in which that cipher group was valid. I cannot say whether there was an underlying basic book with numbered code values enciphered with a three-letter sheet, and my memory is not clear as to the date when this changed to the larger AuKa code book, with numbered code values disguised by three-figure encipherment. The three-figure encipher sheets represented a radical departure, and I believe it took place before my secondment to a new micro-section under George Tatam, charged with processing AuKa traffic intercepted in the Middle East from Luftwaffe units operating in southern Russia and to a lesser extent on the more remote central and northern Russian Fronts.

The AuKa code book was made up of sections. There was provision for single and double figures, so that the use of 'Verfugs' to stand for numbers ceased. There were expanded sections for aircraft types, ship types, nationalities, flight details, weather conditions and emergencies affecting the aircraft and crew. There, the 'Verfugs' were retained.

The effect of the daily-changing encipherment was drastic. Suddenly it became necessary to do in 24 hours all the processing previously done over four weeks. Until then the initial processing of the day's take of German air–ground traffic had been the preserve of RAF Cheadle in Cheshire, whilst the air–ground party at BP merely merged in recoveries from traffic received late after interception in the Middle East. It now became necessary to concentrate processing at BP, where a combined party incorporating both Service and Air Ministry civilian staff from Cheadle, in addition to some of the BP personnel, was organised in three eight-hour watches. As soon after midnight as a radio operator at an intercept site took down a message, it was instantly relayed to our watch, where the cipher groups were recorded on large sheets and the message studied and any possible decodes noted. Gradually, as the day advanced, the day's sheet (actually a large piece of card) was filled in as far as possible, varying with the amount of activity on the part of the Luftwaffe. The watchroom had telephone contact with Cheadle and other intercept sites, and the controller of the watch could request extra cover of a frequency which was producing interesting material.

The next development was the introduction of the 'reciprocal' feature. Originally the three-figure encipher sheet had been accompanied by a corresponding decipher sheet. The former was used to turn the basic code group, let us say 012,

into its cipher equivalent 234. The number 234 in the encipher sheet equated to some other number like 579. So to read
a message enciphered in this system, you also needed a decipher sheet which listed against 234 its equivalent clear-code
value, 012. The Luftwaffe signals bosses now decided to make
the table reciprocal, so that if 012 = 234, then 234 = 012, and
so with every pair. It may have saved paper and have advan-
tages for the radio operator in the cramped aircraft, but it also
proved of great benefit to our analysts.

Henceforth, every recovery worked in reverse as well. If we
recovered 012 as Me-109 in the day's setting of Auka, and we
knew from our recently obtained copy of the AuKa code book
that the AuKa-ese for Me-109 was 234, we then knew that
wherever in our day's traffic we found a cipher group 234 it
must equate to plain-code value 012. Whether we knew what
012 meant already, or had no idea what it meant, we could still
make that equation. We could index occurrences of 012 over
a period and compare the circumstances and perhaps make a
guess at what meaning would fit all the occurrences. On occasions when an aircraft is shot down and an intact cipher sheet
came into our hands, we could thus decipher every three-
figure group in the entire day's traffic, converting the whole
lot into basic code groups.

Orchestra

The next development proved even more to our advantage.
There were a variety of low-grade codes in use by the Luftwaffe for such purposes as notifying forthcoming aircraft

movements, ordering the switching on or off of radio beacons used to guide aircraft back to base (or to their target), monitoring Allied air raids by listening to radar transmissions, air–sea rescue and the like. Some authority with a passion for order and regularity decided that all these disparate minor systems should encipher their basic code texts using the daily-changing AuKa sheets.

As soon as we realised what had happened, it became possible to integrate with the AuKa party the small groups who had previously worked on the other lines in isolation. The system as a whole was christened the Orchestra, and its component code systems were retitled as composers, instruments or noises: Bach, Bassoon and Bump, for example. The noises were connected with radar. As before, any member of the BP party making a recovery passed it to the groups working other systems, so that equations between pairs of groups, like 102 and 234 in the example above, could now be played off against several different codes. Some of these were scarcely readable before, but now we could establish for any three-figure number its true place in the code book in each of the different codes. For example, 012 might mean letter 'A' in one; 'take-off at … hours' in another; and '500 metres' in a third.

A further spin-off was that we could now look back at all earlier occurrences of a particular code group in one code, and we would find that a meaning suggested for it either fitted in with the section of the code book that it was now seen to fall in – or it did not, in which case we had to reject the meaning suggested earlier. The Orchestra did not instantly solve all problems and enable us to read every code in its entirety, because some codes were used for very limited purposes of a technical nature, and we had never seen a captured book and so could only guess at its contents. But it did contribute greatly to the speed with which we could recover the day's AuKa cipher sheets and read systems still of interest. As the war progressed and the Allies gained the upper hand, the Luftwaffe ceased to be a serious threat, but on occasion its desperate operations were still frustrated by our interception and ability to read Orchestral messages.

Imaginary example of messages from Luftwaffe reconnaissance plane using AuKa-type code with three-figure encipherment

To give some idea of the effect of enciphering the basic code groups of messages, and how this made it harder to break the code, we give here two typical but imaginary messages. First of all we show the message preamble, which typically contains the serial number of the message, the number of groups it contains, so that the recipient can check if he has received it in full, and the time at which it was originated. The first line contains the plain text, translated into English, and is broken up into phrases as the radio operator might have encoded them, given the way the code was made up.

Below is the series of three-figure code groups into which the message is converted. Notice how the code condenses some parts of the message thanks to the code being designed to express precisely this kind of data. Underneath each code group we put its equivalent in the imaginary encipher setting of the day or period.

The first message is a routine position report followed by details of the weather conditions found there. The second message came rather soon afterwards, and we supposed that the crew had spotted a convoy of a considerable number of freighters and tankers escorted by warships. This message was sent to give immediate early warning, and any weather report from the new area was held over for a later message.

Message one: group count sixteeen, time of origin 0635

My position is square	7	13	52	3	Weather
102	011	017	048	007	201
651	220	459	973	059	743

Cloud	5 (tenths)	Base	2000	Visibility	15 [km]
202	009	203	135	214	019
088	673	080	490	832	361

Wind direction	South-east	Wind strength	5 [metres/second]
217	324	218	009
079	600	484	673

Message two: group count twenty, time of origin 0651

My position is square	71	34	6	9
102	075	038	010	013
651	490	444	529	096

Convoy	1	Cruiser	4	Destroyers	7
751	005	733	008	736	011
216	882	131	619	353	220

Freighter(s) 5–10000 tons	5	Freighter(s) 10–15000 tons	6	Tankers
767	009	773	010	776
086	673	105	529	400

Heading	South-east	Speed [knots]	10
786	324	787	014
799	600	103	818

It is easy to see that the encoded numbers stand out, all begin with '0', and it would be simple to work out the arrangement and reconstruct the whole lot. In the same way, in the basic code book the weather elements are all in the 200s and the shipping in the 700s. So the basic code has to be enciphered to destroy these obvious features. A random substitution will still show the same group where, for instance, figures such as '1', '2' and '10' recur, but there is nothing obvious to indicate that they are figures, and the evident sequence of the clear code 004, 005, 006 . . . for '1', '2', '3' . . . and so on disappears.

When the encipher sheets were made reciprocal, we were once more able to relate the cipher group to the basic code equivalent. Whenever a recovery was made, and the meaning of a cipher group in a message identified, we could equate the cipher and code groups if we held a captured copy of the code book, and then apply that equation to every occurrence of either group.

When the Orchestra system was introduced, the same advantage for us was multiplied. If we discovered that in a message using code Piccolo a cipher group, say 001, had a certain meaning, and we knew the basic-code equivalent in Piccolo was 335, we could search the day's traffic in all the orchestral codes. Wherever either 001 or 335 appeared, we could then confidently decipher that group to basic code 335 or 001 as the case might be. This meant that code books could be rapidly reconstructed on their true base, and the make-up of the code book became clear. The connections disguised by encipherment, like the numbering of all the weather terms in the page with groups starting with '2' in the imaginary example above, were restored, gradually and only partially where there was little material to work on, but enough to advance our work a great deal.

Appendix 2

Control Commission (British Element),
1946–7

WHEN THE ALLIED FORCES overran Germany and Austria at the end of the Second World War, those countries were divided into zones of occupation: the Russians took roughly the areas east of the Elbe and part of Austria, while the British zone of Germany covered the north-west part. The military government set up to replace the dismantled Nazi apparatus had to restore order and get essential services going again in the devastated cities. It also had the long-term aim of preparing gradually for an eventual handover to a democratic German administration.

Because the German government had ceased to exist, its functions passed to the Allied military forces. They delegated the civil administration to the CCG (Control Commission in Germany), which was charged with carrying out the policies worked out in advance. The CCG in each zone fulfilled its task in different ways. In the British zone, as in the others, the CCG was dependent on the army for assigning requisitioned accommodation in suitable locations, for rations and security. Units were provided with transport. David's unit was given a 15-cwt truck, a Mercedes for the CO with a German driver as well as a Volkswagen for general use. Fuel had to be drawn from army depots.

CCG personnel wore navy-blue battledress uniform with shoulder flashes appropriate to rank and a peaked cap. Uniform was necessary to distinguish them from German civilians, who wore whatever they could acquire. People not yet discharged from the forces still wore military uniforms. There were some parallels between David's unit and the 'contractors' with the American forces in Iraq who have recently been in the public eye for their operating methods. The only people in Germany under British occupation who might have been similarly categorised were the interrogators at the Combined Services Detailed Interrogation Centre at Nenndorf. Interrogations in David's unit were rarely hostile or aggressive, and never physical. It soon became plain to him that the Germans would never have dreamed of tolerating the BP set-up, with its motley crew of untidy civilians, weird, shambling intellectuals or scruffy dons alongside neatly uniformed Service personnel. In the Fatherland, punctilious salutes and impeccable uniform would have been *de rigueur*.

The Intelligence Division of CCG (BE) (the Control Commission's British Element) had to nip in the bud any regrowth of Nazism. It was also charged with carrying out the policies agreed between the four Allied powers for Denazification and Demilitarisation. At the war's end members of the Wehrmacht had been collected in prison camps, and civilians as well as soldiers were screened to see whether they were members of the SS (*Schutzstaffel*) and other organisations declared criminal at Nuremberg. Special war-crimes teams searched for, arrested and questioned suspected war criminals, who were brought to trial if sufficient evidence was found. Such people were classed as Category I, subject to mandatory arrest.

Category II comprised Nazis or militarists considered dangerous to orderly development of democratic government; they were to be held in internment camps. Category III was for persons posing a lesser threat, for release under restrictions to ensure that they should not occupy positions of influence. Category IV covered people whose involvement in Nazi or militaristic activities was minor or who were considered to have reformed their ideas so far as to warrant release under milder restrictions. Finally Category V comprised proven anti-Nazis and pro-Allied persons, to be released unconditionally.

The German GS (General Staff) was the brains of the military machine. It was made up of officers, usually selected in the rank of major for their outstanding intellect, personality and professional aptitude. After thorough training at a college, covering every aspect of war, including industry and economics, the graduate was entitled to put the letters 'iG' after his rank and to wear the red stripe down his uniform trousers. He was then assigned to a post in one or other of three main lines: operation, supply or Intelligence, usually at first at divisional level. He was frequently moved to a different post, so that senior GS officers had wide-ranging experience at all levels of command as well as in front-line troops and headquarters. A posting abroad as military attaché might give him opportunities to study methods and ideas in foreign forces.

Through studying and serving together, numbers of the GS Corps knew each other well and permeated the entire structure of the German armed forces. The navy and the air force had their own separate staffs. Some members of the GS had become hostile to Hitler early on, but as the staff officers, like all German soldiers, had been made to swear an oath of loyalty to the Führer, their ideals of duty towards the head of state prevented many from doing anything to stop him. A group which had cautiously contacted civilian opponents of the Nazis did make several attempts to assassinate him, culminating in the bomb plot of 20 July 1944 by Stauffenberg. Its failure led to the arrest and execution of most of the participants, and caused Hitler to distrust the senior officers. The doctrine of Demilitarisation adopted after the Potsdam Agreement, in 1945, demanded the total dismantling of the German GS, and the exclusion of its members from positions of influence.

David began in November 1946 with a course in Int. Div. HQ in Herford, Westphalia. Like many small German towns away from the industrial bombing targets, Herford was untouched, though, like every place in the western zones, it was crowded with refugees, and the population lived in cold lodgings on short rations. The army and CCG organisations had commandeered large hotels, spa buildings, castles and mansions for their offices and clubs, where their staffs lived in warmth and comfort, with ample food and drink and recreational

facilities. In the new year (1947), David was then posted to
Nine R&IS (Review and Interrogation Staff) at Munster Lager, a former German army camp in the desolate Lüneburger
Heide, part of which now housed the Wehrmacht generals
and staff officers in British captivity. They were guarded by
British and Polish troops. R&IS had its offices and other ranks'
billet in a villa near the camp, but the officers and NCO interrogators lived a mile or so to the west, in a small inn, the
Lindenkrug. The weather was bitterly cold, and David arrived
one evening after a long drive in a 15cwt truck, which had
picked him up at a railhead. He was chilled to the bone despite
his uniform and greatcoat. Stepping into the cosy little bar he
was warmed but taken aback by an unexpected atmosphere.
There was a haze of cigarette smoke and a welcome fug from
the tiled stove, round which half a dozen people were yelling
at the tops of their voices, in all kinds of accents. It sounded
like a riot, but was merely a friendly argument.

The unit was immensely cosmopolitan. The CO, Major
Peter Nettler, was a tall, bespectacled German-Jewish refugee
originally from the Suedetenland in Czechoslovakia. He spoke
perfect English, even though only twenty years old. Another
Czech, Sergeant Tony Haas, was a small man in his thirties.
Sergeant John P was an Austrian who had got to England in
1938, was interned as an enemy alien when war broke out and
shipped to Australia on the notorious *Dunehra*. He was released, volunteered for the army and fought as a tank gunner
against the Afrika Korps as well as in Europe. John P spoke
excellent English with a Cockney accent. He had married

his German girlfriend when she became pregnant. Another Czech–Jewish sergeant was called Frankie. This stooping, flat-footed and shambling character had a pretty German wife and kept a German shepherd pup, which was far from being house-trained. John P christened it 'Pinkus' (*pinkeln* was the German word for 'piddle'), which greatly incensed Frankie.

Captain Henry Mendes came from Amsterdam. He was a mild man whose strong Dutch accent made words like 'Volkswagen' sound like 'Foluksvaage'. A British element was supplied by Bill, a raucous, large-moustached Glaswegian who had been a racing mechanic and a member of the Palestine police, and had an unrivalled command of obscene vituperation. There were also two English officers who never did any work. One spent all his time on the telephone, trying to arrange for his Austrian fiancée to travel from Vienna to the UK. The other was an elderly captain in the Indian army who was awaiting demob. He sat in an armchair reading *The Times*, unmoved by the volatile Continental uproar all round him. Even when the young Pole accidentally discharged a revolver into the floor very near his foot, he remarked calmly, 'Good boy; you missed me.'

The large Jewish element made for colourful conversation, full of Yiddish and German expressions. The motto of the Pioneer Corps, in which many Jews had served, appeared as 'Vy vorry, ve vill vin.' Comments on the difficulties and injustices of post-war life were many: *Auch das noch!* (on top of everything else); *Das hat uns gerade noch gefehlt!* (just what we didn't need); *Da sind wir noch einmal bedient!* (there we are in the soup again) and its answer *Und diesmal erst recht!* (and how!). The final response to any argument vehemently disagreed with was *Bist meschugge geworden?* (are you crazy?).

The CCG needed fluent German speakers who knew something about the country and the Nazis, so naturally they recruited many Jewish refugees. David thought most of the interrogators fair enough in their treatment of the Germans they had to review, though some were rudely treated and abused if they turned out to have been connected with unpleasant incidents in their past.

None of the staff officers waiting to be interrogated seemed to have been associated with the conspiracy to assassinate Hitler, and none made any claim to have been involved. This was not surprising, since in the first place the conspirators had to proceed with infinite caution in sounding out likely sympathisers, before giving them any inkling of their plans. Only a very few in key positions had actually been in the know. Secondly, the Gestapo had reacted with ruthless thoroughness, urged on by the vengeful Führer, in rounding up, questioning, torturing and executing all suspects, even in some cases extirpating their entire families, so that there were few survivors.

David was quite surprised when his CO one day handed him a file, saying that it would be a straightforward case, for his superiors in Intelligence Division HQ had told him that this was an anti-Nazi, and therefore a clear case for release under Category V. General B was a short, middle-aged man whose file was unrevealing, so David took him through his *Fragebogen* (questionnaire) in the usual way. He had been born to an upper-class family in north-east Germany, and had joined the new German Air Force. He had risen early on in a very specialised field, that of close battlefield reconnaissance as an essential part of air–ground co-operation, which had made the blitzkrieg so successful. It was no surprise that he had not connected with the Stauffenberg plot, since the Luftwaffe was barely involved in this. David asked him what he had done to merit the designation of anti-Nazi. He replied that this was all made clear in his diaries, kept all through the war, and now deposited in his bank. The interview was adjourned, and the diaries sent for; they consisted of ten years of jottings, and took hours to scan and digest. There was also a cutting from a Nazi journal, setting out General B's family tree as a pattern of racial purity. His ancestors had been soldiers, parsons and landowners in the Baltic region, and there had not been the least taint of Jewish blood for three hundred years. This hardly sounded like an anti-Nazi background.

He had recorded innumerable meetings with important people, both civil and military, German and foreign, such as Count Galeazzo Ciano and other Italian politicians. Also, just before the invasions of Yugoslavia and Greece, he had person-ally flown over the terrain his pilots would have had to oper-ate over. He had met Reichs Youth Leader Artur Axmann in the last days before the end of the war. David put him down as a careerist who was an expert in his own minor field, but had found himself marooned on his relatively lonely pinnacle. He wrote a specially detailed report, quoting items from the diaries, recommending that General B be kept in Category II, since he was trying to secure release under favourable conditions, on what looked like spurious grounds. After reading the papers and diaries himself, Peter Nettler agreed, and forwarded the report with the file to Int. Div. HQ.

The response was immediate. General B was to be released forthwith under Category V unconditionally. No grounds were given, and the file was never seen again. This decision contributed to the general disillusionment which made David decline to renew his contract with CCG at the end of the year. Forty years later, while reading Peter Wright's *Spycatcher*, a name rang a bell in his memory. (Now, reader, you thought I was exaggerating about David's phenomenal memory, but here he is instantly remembering a name only once mentioned in a file read forty years earlier among dozens of other files!) The name that had struck him was zu Putlitz, and he at once remembered it as being the name of the Prussian baron whose farm had been managed by General B! This Putlitz had been First Secretary at the German Legation in London before the war, and had in 1935, through the intervention of Peter Ustinov's father, been introduced to Winston Churchill, and began to supply MI5 (the counter-espionage organ of British intelligence) with first-class Intelligence about German rearmament.

At the outbreak of war, Putlitz was air attaché at the German Embassy in Holland, from which Ustinov risked his life to extricate him, having learned that the Gestapo were closing in on him. He was brought to London and confided to the care of Anthony Blunt, who had joined MI5 and was later unmasked as the Fourth Man of the group of Russian spies composed of Guy Burgess, Donald Maclean and Kim Philby. According to Peter Wright, Blunt and Putlitz were lovers during the war. After the war Putlitz chose to return to his native area of eastern Germany, now under Russian occupation, and Blunt personally escorted him to the checkpoint and saw him across the border.

Probably Putlitz had been a Russian agent all along, and only incidentally helped the British. Somebody high up in the CCG evidently overruled the decision about General B, since Int. Div. was essentially an offshoot of MI5, and Philby had taken control of MI5's Russian Section in 1944. Evidently General B's claim to be anti-Nazi and pro-British was connected to his employer's activities, or perhaps to the fact that he himself had from time to time supplied information to foreign powers. These facts would have been impossible to divulge in 1947. Probably his release was procured by Putlitz's pals Blunt and Philby, and General B most likely joined Putlitz in the Russian zone. David's distrust of the man seemed to have been well founded.

From time to time CCG had visitors, usually members of the war-crimes teams of various nationalities, looking for men in the camp. One of these visitors was a Yugoslavian called Sliviç, a small mild man who always brought with him bottles of Slivoviç (plum brandy), so that it was difficult to remember which was the man and which the liqueur. Extradition to Yugoslavia was a fate the Germans dreaded more than anything, since hideous rumours circulated about the fearsome vengeance exacted by Tito's partisans, which were now in power.

The inmates of the camp were sure that no one ever came back alive from their clutches.

Once a gaunt, cadaverous German in drab clothes came to the office one dark night and was closeted with the CO for some time before slinking furtively out again. It appeared that this was a former Gestapo agent who was being infiltrated into the Eastern zone, the border not being at that period as heavily fortified as it was later to become. The man had been having a final briefing, and returned some weeks later for debriefing. The other interrogators did not know who controlled these clandestine operations, and did not in any case want to step outside their prescribed functions.

Suddenly a team of Counter-Intelligence Service agents descended upon the unit, taking over the office and crowding into the mess. They were carrying out part of a synchronised action over all three Western zones, to seize the ringleaders of a small-scale neo-Nazi movement which had been detected and watched for some time. The intruders were tough, brash, swaggering young men, all Jewish, with unmannerly and overbearing ways. It took them only a few days to round up and quell this feeble stirring of Nazi sentiment after the war.

In accordance with urgent directives from HQ, Munster Lager was to be wound up in the spring, so intensive efforts were required by all interrogators, supported by a bevy of typists specially drafted in. It was at this time that David went on a visit to Hamburg, which consisted mainly of shattered ruins and heaps of rubble, from which every morning clean, neatly dressed children emerged on their way to school. There was a story current that one day four men had walked into that world-renowned hotel the Four Seasons – then an officers' club – and had politely asked the officers standing round the bar to step aside while they rolled up the magnificent long carpet and carried it away.

From Munster Lager David was sent to Adelheide, near Bremen, where Category II detainees were now living in a comfortable modern Luftwaffe camp, heated by a central furnace fed from a conveyor belt with powdered peat, which abounded in that flat swampy country. A new policy directed that the detainees should speedily be let go after a further review. The 'customers', who had an efficient news network, soon understood this, and the atmosphere was relatively friendly, with one unpleasant exception. This was a gigantic Bavarian with a harsh accent, who had been formerly processed at Munster Lager as a full staff general. He absolutely refused to discuss his political opinions, past or present, resolutely maintaining that he had never had any, being completely occupied with his soldierly duties and his great hobby, which was playing Mozart violin quartets. The interrogators were in a hurry, and David simply wrote a report stating that this was a staff officer of extraordinary experience and formidable personality, who avoided disclosing his outlook and was able to cause great trouble; he should therefore be kept in Category II. The Review Board agreed, and the general found himself on his way to Adelheide.

One day a briefing came through that the US Army were recruiting German staff officers to 'write history' (that is, to pass on their experience of warfare against the Soviets). Every officer was to be interviewed and invited in confidence to volunteer for this interesting and comfortable assignment, with family quarters provided. Of course in stalked the Herr General, who wasted no time in making it clear that he would not volunteer for anything at all. So overwhelming was his towering presence and his barely controlled animosity that David was relieved when he stormed out without offering open insults or violence, and felt that his original assessment was entirely justified.

During this period David was sent with a colleague, Oskar Hamm, to the far north of Scotland, to process a camp full of Nazi fanatics and troublemakers who had been weeded out from POW (Prisoner of War) camps in Canada, America and elsewhere for such things as complicity in lynching suspected stool-pigeons. The camp was at Watten near Wick. Oskar was a lawyer from Cologne who had escaped to England; he was a man of high principles and great humanity. In the camp, however, they came up for the first time against the true face of Nazism undisguised. A surprising number of the inmates were steadfast, unrepentant, arrogant Nazis, some of whom refused to believe that the war was over and Hitler dead, declaring that these were Allied propaganda lies. Some were truculent and ranted furiously; others were polite and rational, but advanced doctrines like the survival of the fittest or 'my country, right or wrong' as justification for Nazi policies.

One burly German sergeant major stamped into the room, bawled out his name and rank, and then asked, civilly enough, to see David's ID. When he saw a British passport, he screamed that such a man should be ashamed to be associating with Jews and keeping honest men in captivity after the war was over. It was plain that even the most rabid of these men would change their tune once they experienced the reality of post-war Germany under Allied occupation, or else would be laughed at by the population, and that hardly any of them had enough military skills to be a threat. To the surprise and dismay of the camp staff, Oskar and David recommended that all the inmates should be released as soon as possible, and they flew back to Adelheide.

One of the English admin. staff there was a former NCO in the army who had officiated as executioner after the Nuremberg trials, and could not stop describing his macabre experiences. It was not only the defeated in that war who had suffered psychological damage.

David's last posting in the CCG was to Senne Lager near Bielefeld, a former Wehrmacht training camp on a flat heath close to the East–West autobahn, which ran over the Teutoburger Wald hills, from where wide views could be seen. He was entitled to live in the officers' mess, but if he did so the CO's mistress, a lady of very strange antecedents, would have had to move into her lover's bedroom. So, not to eradicate moral turpitude but merely the appearance of moral turpitude, David accepted living quarters in the sergeants' mess.

His last months were spent perfunctorily interviewing ex-Nazis of all kinds before their release. One in particular was memorable. A dark, handsome man of about forty, Gunther d'Alquen was an SS colonel, and had been editor of the official journal of that body, *Schwarze Korps* (Black Corps). He had obviously been a leading and influential member of the Nazi movement. However, his editorials during the last year of the war had taken on an increasingly realistic tone, verging on defeatism. It was strange that he got away with such views at a time when Hitler and Goebbels demanded absolute conformity with the official party line, namely that Germany could still win the war, even when the Russians were on the Oder and the western Allies on the Rhine. People were arrested and shot for merely voicing doubts.

But, now, d'Alquen took the line that Nazi Germany was an attempt to set up what he called a *nationaler Zweckstaat*, which David interpreted as something like a national state as be-all and end-all, the creation of which outweighed every other consideration. It had failed, so now the Germans had to throw themselves into working with the Allies. This was quite a widespread attitude, but naturally its proponents were not anxious to discuss the crimes and devastation which were the outcome of these ideas. However, d'Alquen possessed an agile mind, a fluent tongue and a strong personality, which showed how he had acquired his former position. He was not known to have been involved with any specific war crimes, so he was recommended for discharge. However his vicar-of-Bray-like propensity to change with ease to the winning side did not say a great deal for his integrity.

Another curious encounter was with an elderly colonel in the Abwehr, who had in the First World War been associated in some way with the German High Command's cryptographic department. Speaking of those days to David, the colonel mentioned with great respect a certain *Väterlein* (little father), who could actually solve cyphers without knowing in what language the messages were encrypted. That name was pronounced in German almost identically with Fetterlein, and David was sure that it was Ernst, the father, who was recalled with such awe. It was strange to him to remember among the ruins and wreckage of post-war Germany the quiet corridor in F Block where the younger Fetterlein would greet his father so affectionately.

David had another reminder of Bletchley when he ran into Ted D, who had been in Mr B's section. He was a small thin Cockney, with the hollow cheeks that were evidence of an undernourished childhood. He had run away from home at fourteen and made his way to the continent, where he picked up several languages. Ted D was cheerful and witty, but he evidently wondered why his life had been so different from the rather privileged lives of many of his fellow workers. However, when David met him, he had no complaints. He had joined the CCG, become a Kreis resident officer, married a German lady and now revelled in the life of a country squire, shooting deer and wild boar, and carousing with the local farmers. Never was a change of circumstance so well deserved.

After a year in the Control Commission David was sickened by the chaos, corruption and exploitation he saw all round him, and returned to England and the work for which he was so superbly fitted, in GCHQ. He had come full circle; he was to work with some of the people he had known at BP, and un-der much the same conditions of absolute secrecy.

For many of the rest of us, it was a wrench to leave that atmosphere and so many friends, now widely separated. This book is therefore not only a recollection of but also a tribute to those friends and to that unforgettable time. BP was not, of course, a Garden of Eden. We were all human there, with the usual faults and failings, but most people were so friendly and so good-natured, so willing to help that it was a wonder-ful place for an ignorant young person to grow up and to find friends of all ages and with every kind of passionate interest.

Appendix 3
Food at Bletchley

THROUGHOUT HIS NOVEL *Enigma*, Mr Harris describes the food at Bletchley Park, and indeed in the Britain of 1943, as 'vile' and 'disgusting'. In fact it was neither, and it's difficult to see where he got this idea. I suppose he thought that as so many convoys were being destroyed, food must necessarily be short, but why should that mean that it was badly cooked? Wartime rationing was extremely good. It was remarked on all sides that the pre-war slum children – rickety, malnourished and often tubercular – were never seen during the war. Their parents all had well-paid jobs in factories or the Services, and could for the first time afford to feed their children properly. Babies had free, vitaminised dried milk, free orange juice and rosehip syrup. Children under five had blue ration books, which entitled them to first go at any rare food such as fresh oranges. Those living alone, with one ration book, sometimes went a little short if they liked drinking a great deal of tea or were fond of butter. But there were hotel meals for those who could afford it, British Restaurants where the food was very good and cheap, and fried fish and chips, which were off the ration though you had to queue, and the sign 'frying tonight' appeared only on certain nights. The food was nearly always well cooked, if plain, and rations distributed with scrupulous honesty. No one ever went without, and the Black Market was, in general, looked upon with detestation. Offal was not on the ration, but was scarce. Still, your butcher might slip a pair of kidneys into your weekly meat parcel if you had a son coming home on leave. Some of the meat ration had to be taken in corned beef, but households with several ration books managed a joint on Sundays, served cold with jacket potatoes on Monday and the remains minced to make a cottage pie (largely potato) on Tuesday. The great difficulty for the housewife, unless she had a husband with an allotment, was that onions, for some reason never fully understood, became like gold dust in the last years of the war. If a greengrocer produced one for you secretly from under the counter, you were enjoined to keep it secret. All Ministry of Food recipes and pamphlets in those years had the rubric 'take one onion (if available).'

In 1942 (when Mr Harris's Jericho was working at Bletchley Park) dried egg came in from America, and you were entitled to a one shilling and nine pence tin, containing the essence of twelve eggs, as well as your fresh egg entitlement. This, if you added chopped parsley or chives, made palatable omelettes and scrambled egg, and was very useful in puddings, cakes and savoury dishes. Then, too, in 1944, when Admiral Doenitz had withdrawn his 'wolf packs' and the convoys

could sail free, South Africa sent Britain a cargo of four pound
tins of jam and marmalade. This was never put on the ration,
but was shared out among hotels, restaurants and boarding-
houses, where you might be surprised by grapefruit marmalade with your breakfast or pineapple jam with your scones.

During the war years Britain became a nation of savers.
Everything was recycled: paper, rags, tins, old tyres and wel-
lington boots – even bones, after having been boiled for stock
or soup, were used by the government for some mysterious
purpose. Tennis courts and rose gardens were dug up to grow
vegetables. Everyone who could had an allotment, and every
kind of berry was harvested. Parties of schoolchildren and
members of the WVS (Women's Voluntary Services) scoured
the countryside, gathering sloes, elderberries, blackberries,
crab apples, hips and haws, rowan berries and mushrooms. All
were dried, bottled, pulped or made into syrups, jellies, jams,
pickles and chutneys, with the co-operation of the Ministry
of Food, which allocated extra sugar for these activities and
actually issued a leaflet (one of many, on every conceivable
subject) called *Hedgerow and Harvest*. The whole nation, in
fact, was better fed than it had ever been.

But you would never guess this from *Enigma*. Food in the
book is horrible everywhere. I go thoughtfully through the list
of BP survivors, and I wonder which one pulled Mr Harris's
leg so unmercifully. Or did he just assume, with so many convoys being sunk in 1942, that food must be scarce? But why
should it also be badly cooked? It never was. Cooks in the
Services were well trained, and housewives became dexterous

at making the best use of their rations. But Mr Harris has determined that tea and bread were 'grey'. Actually, many people kept a teapot with used tea leaves stewing on the hob, until the ensuing drink was dark brown and tasted of pure tannin; or, if you just poured boiling water on the used tea leaves, you had a pale brown liquid which, if you ever had a lemon, could have been mistaken for *thé citron*; but I never saw 'grey' tea.

Bread was always good, and, although you could obtain white bread throughout the war, in 1941 the Ministry of Food introduced a 'national' loaf, consisting of the whole corn (what we now know as wholemeal bread). This was not very popular at first, but it was good and nourishing, and was gradually accepted by all but the most finicky eaters. So there was no need for Jericho to give Wigram a slice of 'greyish' bread. Nor would he have needed to use a 'smear' of margarine on his toast. If he had had a smear of anything in his pantry, it would have been of his own personal ration of butter, which was always meticulously given to everyone in colleges, boarding-houses or other places of residence. To take another person's butter without permission was regarded as treachery – a terrible misdemeanour. To complete Wigram's entertainment, Jericho scraped mould from a pot of 'pre-war' jam. But jam or marmalade was plentiful, and available for quite a small number of 'points' (the small detachable sections of the ration book with which you could buy extra foods such as biscuits, preserves and currants).

We have no space here to discuss Mr Harris's descriptions of the appalling food supplied by Jericho's landlady, since no landlady that I met or heard of either hoarded or supplied bad food, but his references to the BP canteen and the food supplied there are quite untrue. His description of the canteen is that it was 'as big as an aircraft hangar, brightly lit and thunderously noisy . . . The din was dreadful, and so was the smell . . . of cabbage and boiled fish and custard, laced with cigarette smoke and damp clothes.'

In reality, the BP canteen had been finished in 1942, and was a pleasant place – not at all like an aircraft hangar – but well lit in winter and lavishly windowed and sunny in summer, smelling, if at all, of good well-cooked food. Why should it smell of damp clothes? People had umbrellas and waterproofs, which they could hang up near the entrance. I never remember it as being particularly noisy. People spoke quietly, and many played with pocket chess sets or read newspapers or magazines. There was just a pleasant hum of conversation.

On one side of the room as you entered was a long counter with crockery and cutlery at the top, which you put on your tray, and then walked along the counter selecting your meal. There was no serving hatch, and indeed Mr Harris cannot have worked out how the five or six hundred people he visualises queuing for food could possibly be served at a single hatch. First of all on the counter were rectangular dishes containing salads. Many of these, to the young British person who had never been abroad, were exotic to a degree: sweetcorn, olives, Russian and Waldorf salads, all kinds of mixed vegetables and dressing, surprising to the eye accustomed to a salad comprising a few lettuce leaves, a sliced tomato and some beetroot. In winter there were soups instead of some of the salads. Then came the main dishes, always two and sometimes three, with a good selection of vegetables, with cheese, nut or rice dishes for vegetarians. There was always a choice of two sweets, hot or cold, and I believe a cup of something claiming to be coffee could be obtained.

There was no way in which Jericho could have been simply handed a plate of 'boiled potatoes in a curdled yellow grease and . . . a slab of something ribbed and grey 'which tasted like fishy liver or congealed cod-liver oil'. It was whale meat, which Jericho stigmatised as 'perfectly vile'. In fact, since whales are mammals and don't feed on fish, it was of a thick texture, like turbot, snowy white and rather tasteless and chewy. Many Bletchleyites even then objected to the slaughter of whales, and it was removed from the menu. Iceland sent us fresh-salted cod, which appeared as 'baked cod', 'creamed cod', 'cod provençale' and 'curried cod'.

Jericho also ate, at the same meal, 'some kind of' fruit tart, which tasted like cardboard. In fact the pastry cook at BP was extremely good, and when I was there, a few months after the egregious Jericho is supposed to have left, this cook produced gooseberry pies which even code-breakers who never ate sweets queued for.

And because he had been bundled back to Cambridge (having been proved to be a traitor), Jericho missed the 1943 Christmas dinner for Huts Four and Eight, given by Frank Birch. 'The tables were positively groaning with Christmas fare. They were arranged in a T-shape. The top of the "T" was loaded with turkey, geese and chicken, while the table down the centre at which we all sat was decorated with a game pie, and fruit salad, cheese and various other dishes.' Oh well. Jericho probably wouldn't have appreciated it anyway.

Select Bibliography

Ballard, Geoffrey *On Ultra Active Service*, Spectrum Publications, Richmond, Australia, 1991.

Bennett, Ralph *Behind the Battle; Intelligence in the War with Germany, 1939–1945*, Sinclair-Stevenson, London, 1994.

Calvocoressi, Peter *Top Secret Ultra*, Cassell, London, 1980.

Fitzgerald, Penelope *The Knox Brothers*, Macmillan, London, 1977.

Harris, Robert *Enigma*, Arrow, London, 1995.

Hinsley, F. H. and Stripp, Alan (eds) *Codebreakers: The Inside Story of Bletchley Park*, OUP, Oxford, 1993.

Smith, Michael *New Cloak, Old Dagger*, Victor Gollancz, London, 1996.

Station X: The Codebreakers of Bletchley Park, Channel 4 Books, Macmillan, London, 1998.

Welchman, Gordon *The Hut Six Story*, Allen Lane, London, 1982.

Winterbotham F. W. *The Ultra Secret*, Weidenfeld and Nicolson, London, 1974.

Glossary

Additive number to be added to disguise a basic code group.

AuKa abbreviation for *Aufklaerungs und Kampfflieger Signalstafel Land und See* (Reconnaissance and Bomber code, Land and Sea).

Call sign (in radiotelephony) a word, name or number, or combination of such, identifying a participant while concealing his identity from hostile ears.

cipher system for disguising a text, whether in plain language or encoded, by cryptographic means, manual or mechanical.

clear, clear text original plain-language text of a message before encoding.

code a system for disguising clear text; common methods for this involve substitution or transposition.

code book a book ranging in size from a couple of pages to dictionary size, containing words, letters, numbers and phrases needed for communications, providing opposite each such element a set of numbers or letters to be substituted for the plain text.

code group a set of such letters or figures drawn from a code book.

code table small code book consisting of a card with clear vocabulary and code equivalents.

code value encoded equivalent of an item in a message.

decipher to remove encipherment from a message, revealing plain text or code.

decode to remove the code concealing clear text.

decrypt as decode; also used for the resulting plain-text message.

D/F (direction finding) locating a transmitter by taking bearings on its maximum and minimum signal strength, measured at several listening sites. The position where the different bearings cross indicates the source of the signal.

encipher, encrypt to disguise plain text, or an encoded text, by applying some systematic alteration either letter by letter or group by group, often by mechanical means.

encode to change plain text into code groups.

frequency radio frequency used for radio or other transmission. Also used when referring to frequency of occurrence of letters, figures or code groups in messages.

intercept to record, manually or mechanically, a radio or other transmission. Also used to mean anything obtained by interception.

krack BP-speak for the result when a cipher group was cracked.

Orchestra name given to a group of Luftwaffe codes which shared a system of encipherment using daily-changing three-digit sheets. Related codes were titled by BP code-breakers using names of composers, musical instruments or noises.

Playfair a code of British origin, in which the alphabet, omitting

'J', was written into a square in a jumbled order, and used to encode pairs of plain text by the opposite corners of the rectangle they formed if on different lines and columns, or by using adjacent letters if on the same line or in the same column. The German forces employed two such squares in conjunction.

preamble information usually prefixed to the text of radio messages, consisting typically of a serial number, the number of groups in the message and the time of origin; and sometimes an indication of priority.

Q-code an internationally accepted code used by radio operators, both civil and military, to convey briefly data about communications, weather, flight or marine details.

radio beacon a medium-frequency transmitter sending out a signal for the navigational guidance of aircraft. Such a beacon near an airfield runway could radiate signals for aircraft to home in on their base in darkness or bad weather.

The Luftwaffe also used a system of high-power directional beacon transmitters to guide bombers to their targets in enemy territory; the navigator flew along one beam until it intersected with another and then released his bombs.

RHN a code group included in the monthly-changing three-letter encipherment used with a predecessor of the Luftwaffe AuKa code; it was in use roughly from mid-1941 to mid-1942. BP analysts used this to designate the series.

speller a message or portion of a message containing plain text encoded letter by letter, resulting in recognisable repetitions of code equivalents of common letters, such as 'e' in English and most European languages.

spoof a spurious message sent either for subscribers to a radio
    net to tune their receivers, or to disguise the absence of genuine
    messages. If there were sudden flurries of messages on a radio
    net, that would alert hostile listeners that operations were
    imminent; hence the Germans tried to maintain a regular flow
    of messages.

substitution replacing a plain-language letter, figure or phrase
    with a code group, or a different letter or figure, in some pre-
    arranged way.

traffic messages sent over a radio circuit.

transposition changing the order of components of a message in a
    pre-arranged systematic manner before transmission.

Y service an organisation of RAF, naval and military listening
    posts at suitable locations for interception of German military,
    naval or air signals using voice radiotelephony. This was done by
    expert linguists, mostly female.

Index

Other Greenhill books include:

RED STAR AGAINST THE SWASTIKA
The Story of a Soviet Pilot over the Eastern Front
Vasily B. Emelianenko
ISBN 1-85367-649-7

AT THE HEART OF THE REICH
The Secret Diary of Hitler's Army Adjutant
Major Gerhard Engel
ISBN 1-85367- 655-1

TANK RIDER
Into the Reich with the Red Army
Evgeni Bessonov
ISBN 1-85367-671-3

BLOOD RED SNOW
The Memoirs of a German Soldier on the Eastern Front
Günter K. Koschorrek
ISBN 1-85367-639-X

LUFTWAFFE OVER AMERICA
The Secret Plans to Bomb the United States in World War II
Manfred Griehl
ISBN 1-85367-608-X

THE RECONSTRUCTION OF WARRIORS
Archibald McIndoe, the Royal Air Force and the Guinea Pig Club
E. R. Mayhew
ISBN 1-85367-610-1

Greenhill offers selected discounts and special offers on books ordered directly from us. For more information on our books please visit www.greenhillbooks.com. You can also write to us at Park House, 1 Russell Gardens, London NW11 9NN, England.